MYSTERIES, LEGENDS, AND UNEXPLAINED PHENOMENA

GHOSTS AND HAUNTED PLACES

MYSTERIES, LEGENDS, AND UNEXPLAINED PHENOMENA

MYSTERIES, LEGENDS, AND UNEXPLAINED PHENOMENA

GHOSTS AND HAUNTED PLACES

ROSEMARY ELLEN GUILEY

Consulting Editor: Rosemary Ellen Guiley

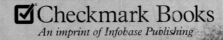
☑Checkmark Books
An imprint of Infobase Publishing

GHOSTS AND HAUNTED PLACES

Checkmark Books
An imprint of Infobase Publishing
132 West 31st Street
New York NY 10001

ISBN-13: 978-1-60413-317-2
ISBN-10: 1-6041-3317-1

Library of Congress has cataloged the hardcover edition as follows:
Guiley, Rosemary.
  Ghosts and haunted places / Rosemary Ellen Guiley.
    p. cm. — (Mysteries, legends, and unexplained phenomena)
  Includes bibliographical references and index.
  ISBN-13: 978-0-7910-9392-4
  ISBN-10: 0-7910-9392-1
  1. Ghosts. 2. Haunted places. I. Title. II. Series.

  BF1461.G86 2008
  133.1—dc22

                    2007032012

Checkmark Books are available at special discounts when purchased in bulk quantities for businesses, associations, institutions, or sales promotions. Please call our Special Sales Department in New York at (212) 967-8800 or (800) 322-8755.

You can find Chelsea House on the World Wide Web at http://www.chelseahouse.com

Text design by James Scotto-Lavino
Cover design by Ben Peterson

Printed in the United States of America

Bang EJB 10 9 8 7 6 5 4 3 2 1

This book is printed on acid-free paper.

All links and Web addresses were checked and verified to be correct at the time of publication. Because of the dynamic nature of the Web, some addresses and links may have changed since publication and may no longer be valid.

Contents

Foreword

Did you ever have an experience that turned your whole world upside down? Maybe you saw a ghost or a UFO. Perhaps you had an unusual, vivid dream that seemed real. Maybe you suddenly knew that a certain event was going to happen in the future. Or, perhaps you saw a creature or a being that did not fit the description of anything known in the natural world. At first you might have thought your imagination was playing tricks on you. Then, perhaps, you wondered about what you experienced and went looking for an explanation.

Every day and night people have experiences they can't explain. For many people these events are life changing. Their comfort zone of what they can accept as "real" is put to the test. It takes only one such experience for people to question the reality of the mysterious worlds that might exist beyond the one we live in. Perhaps you haven't encountered the unknown, but you have an intense curiosity about it. Either way, by picking up this book you've started an adventure to explore and learn more, and you've come to the right place! The book you hold has been written by a leading expert in the paranormal—someone who understands unusual experiences and who knows the answers to your questions.

As a seeker of knowledge, you have plenty of company. Mythology, folklore, and records of the past show that human beings have had paranormal experiences throughout history. Even prehistoric cave paintings and gravesites indicate that early humans had concepts of the supernatural and of an afterlife. Humans have always sought to understand paranormal experiences and to put them into a frame of reference that makes sense to us in our daily lives. Some of the greatest minds in history have grappled with questions about the paranormal. For example, Greek philosopher Plato pondered the nature of dreams and how we "travel" during them. Isaac Newton was interested in the esoteric study of alchemy, which has magical elements, and St. Thomas Aquinas explored the nature of angels and spirits. Philosopher William James joined organizations dedicated to psychical research, and even the inventor of the light bulb, Thomas Alva Edison, wanted to build a device that could talk to the dead. More recently physicists such as David Bohm, Stephen Hawking, William Tiller, and Michio Kaku have developed ideas that may help explain how and why paranormal phenomena happen, and neuroscience researchers like Michael Persinger have explored the nature of consciousness.

Exactly what is a paranormal experience or phenomenon? "Para" is derived from a Latin term for "beyond." So "paranormal" means "beyond normal," or things that do not fit what we experience through our five senses alone and which do not follow the laws we observe in nature and in science. Paranormal experiences and phenomena run the gamut from the awesome and marvelous, such as angels and miracles, to the downright terrifying, such as vampires and werewolves.

Paranormal experiences have been consistent throughout the ages, but explanations of them have changed as societies, cultures, and technologies have changed. For example, our ancestors were much closer to the invisible realms. In times when life was simpler, they saw, felt, and experienced other realities on a daily basis. When night fell, the darkness was thick and quiet, and it was easier to see unusual things, such as ghosts. They had no electricity to keep the night lit up. They had no media for constant communication and entertainment. Travel was difficult. They had more time to notice subtle things that were just beyond their ordinary senses. Few doubted their experiences. They accepted the invisible realms as an extension of ordinary life.

Today we have many distractions. We are constantly busy from the time we wake up until we go to bed. The world is full of light and noise 24 hours a day, seven days a week. We have television, the

Internet, computer games, and cell phones to keep us busy, busy, busy. We are ruled by technology and science. Yet, we still have paranormal experiences very similar to those of our ancestors. Because these occurrences do not fit neatly into science and technology, many people think they are illusions, and there are plenty of skeptics always ready to debunk the paranormal and reinforce that idea.

In roughly the past 100 years, though, some scientists have studied the paranormal and attempted to find scientific evidence for it. Psychic phenomena have proven difficult to observe and measure according to scientific standards. However, lack of scientific proof does not mean paranormal experiences do not happen. Courageous scientists are still looking for bridges between science and the supernatural.

My personal experiences are behind my lifelong study of the paranormal. Like many children I had invisible playmates when I was very young, and I saw strange lights in the yard and woods that I instinctively knew were the nature spirits who lived there. Children seem to be very open to paranormal phenomena, but their ability to have these experiences often fades away as they become more involved in the outside world, or, perhaps, as adults tell them not to believe in what they experience, that it's only in their imagination. Even when I was very young, I was puzzled that other people would tell me with great authority that I did not experience what I knew I did.

A major reason for my interest in the paranormal is precognitive dreaming experienced by members of my family. Precognition means "fore knowing," or knowing the future. My mother had a lot of psychic experiences, including dreams of future events. As a teen it seemed amazing to me that dreams could show us the future. I was determined to learn more about this and to have such dreams myself. I found books that explained extrasensory perception, the knowing of information beyond the five senses. I learned about dreams and experimented with them. I taught myself to visit distant places in my dreams and to notice details about them that I could later verify in the physical world. I learned how to send people telepathic messages in dreams and how to receive messages in dreams. Every night became an exciting adventure.

Those interests led me to other areas of the paranormal. Pretty soon I was engrossed in studying all kinds of topics. I learned different techniques for divination, including the Tarot. I learned how to meditate. I took courses to develop my own psychic skills, and I gave psychic readings to others. Everyone has at least some natural psychic ability and can improve it with attention and practice.

Next I turned my attention to the skies, to ufology, and what might be "out there" in space. I studied the lore of angels and fairies. I delved into the dark shadowy realm of demons and monsters. I learned the principles of real magic and spell casting. I undertook investigations of haunted places. I learned how to see auras and do energy healing. I even participated in some formal scientific laboratory experiments for telepathy.

My studies led me to have many kinds of experiences that have enriched my understanding of the paranormal. I cannot say that I can prove anything in scientific terms. It may be some time yet before science and the paranormal stop flirting with each other and really get together. Meanwhile, we can still learn a great deal from our personal experiences. At the very least, our paranormal experiences contribute to our inner wisdom. I encourage others to do the same as I do. Look first for natural explanations of strange phenomena. If natural explanations cannot be found or seem unlikely, consider paranormal explanations. Many paranormal experiences fall into a vague area, where although a natural cause might exist, we simply don't know what could explain them. In that case I tell people to trust their intuition that they had a paranormal experience. Sometimes the explanation makes itself known later on.

I have concluded from my studies and experiences that invisible dimensions are layered upon our world, and that many paranormal experiences occur when there are openings between worlds. The doorways often open at unexpected times. You take a trip, visit a haunted place, or have a strange dream–and suddenly reality shifts. You get a glimpse behind the curtain that separates the ordinary from the extraordinary.

The books in this series will introduce you to these exciting and mysterious subjects. You'll learn many things that will astonish you. You'll be given lots of tips for how to explore the paranormal on your own. Paranormal investigation is a popular field, and you don't have to be a scientist or a full-time researcher to explore it. There are many things you can do in your free time. The knowledge you gain from these books will help prepare you for any unusual and unexpected experiences.

As you go deeper into your study of the paranormal, you may come up with new ideas for explanations. That's one of the appealing aspects of paranormal investigation–there is always room for bold ideas. So, keep an open and curious mind, and think big. Mysterious worlds are waiting for you!

—Rosemary Ellen Guiley

Introduction

Ghosts attract us like moths to a flame. We want to see ghosts, so we go to haunted places, hoping and daring to be scared. But when we hear the first odd bump, we're off and running—and sometimes screaming.

Ghosts are everywhere: in scary places, scary books, scary movies, and scary stories. Ghosts rank high on the list of things that frighten us, even though we can't resist wondering about them. Is it because we never know exactly when and where they're going to show up—and what they're going to do? Or is it because we feel that they're not supposed to be in our world—that they belong to the world of the dead?

We don't quite know whether or not to believe in ghosts. But even if we don't believe, there comes a time for many people when their eyes and ears tell them differently.

People have been uncertain about ghosts ever since the first ghost stories were recorded. Over the course of history, humans have batted around a lot of ideas about ghosts. Some of these ideas have become part of our folklore, as well as our religious and spiritual beliefs. Science has had an uneasy relationship with ghosts, since ghosts just don't conform to scientific rules. A few plucky scientists who have investigated ghosts have added to our storehouse of knowledge, but still, there is precious little that is certain about ghosts. On the other hand, there are piles of possible explanations and accounts of personal experiences with ghosts.

You probably have a ghost experience or two of your own to share. If you asked your family and friends about their ghost encounters, you'd probably be surprised by the answers you get. A lot of people experience ghosts, but they just don't talk about it much.

The 1990s brought an explosion of interest in ghosts and **hauntings**. Serious interest in the study of the paranormal came out of the shadows and into the mainstream, led by a fascination with ghosts. Especially important were media influences. Dramas on television and in film featured many paranormal themes and elements. Reality television shows such as *Most Haunted* in the United Kingdom and *Ghost Hunters* in the United States riveted audiences every week with their investigations of haunted sites. Ghost research and investigation groups sprang up everywhere. Some grew to considerable size, such as the American Ghost Society, founded by Troy Taylor. Paranormal Web sites multiplied. Ghostvillage.com, founded by Jeff Belanger, became the largest paranormal Web site on the Internet.

Ghosts are a complex subject and a fascinating one to study. They've been stereotyped as filmy white things drifting about graveyards, lonely places, and creepy houses, or as invisible things that like to scare or threaten people. There is some truth in the stereotypes, but ghosts are much more. They are part of a mystery: a mystery about life, death, and the afterlife, and about dimensions beyond the world we know. By studying ghosts, we can explore this mystery.

So let's take a look at the territory this book covers. Along the way, we'll visit some of the most interesting, unusual and famous ghosts and hauntings, including cases you probably aren't familiar with.

Chapter 1, "Dead People Who Don't Go Away," discusses the most favored explanations of different types of ghosts. Both people and animals can become ghosts. Even inanimate objects can take phantom form. The sidebar, "The Top Ten Spookiest Places," gives a list of places where you are most likely to find ghosts. Yes, they do have their favorite "haunts."

Chapter 2, "Now You See 'Em, Now You Don't," explains how people experience ghosts. Note the word "experience." Most people actually never *see* ghosts. But ghosts make themselves known, without a doubt. The sidebar about Resurrection Mary tells the story of a hitchhiking ghost girl who always wants a ride home—to her grave!

Want to know where ghosts really call home? Chapter 3, "Where Do Ghosts Come From?" looks at the leading explanations of the origins of ghosts. Why do some people become ghosts and others not? You'll learn why. Then give some thought to the sidebar, "Are Ghosts Just in Your Head?" Some experts think ghosts are indeed phantoms—but only of the imagination.

Chapter 4, "Screaming Banshees and Death Omen Ghosts," tells about an entire class of ghosts who do nothing but announce death and disaster. Perhaps it is fitting that the dead should be the ones to give the living advance warning that they're about to die. **Banshees** and death omen ghosts are among the most feared in folklore all over the world.

"Battles That Never End" are featured in Chapter 5. Ghost armies and battles are another important class of ghosts. Violent death is prominent in the apparent making of ghosts, and many battlefields are filled with phantoms that replay their battles endlessly. Visitors who happen upon the scenes feel as though they've stepped back into time.

Have you ever lost a pet, but felt the animal was still around? If so, you have plenty of company. Animals become ghosts, too, as you'll learn in Chapter 6, "Animal Ghosts and Phantimals." Besides pets, wild animals become ghosts and continue to haunt the places they roamed while alive. There are even more interesting animal ghosts, the "phantimals." Some are believed to come from the spirit world, never having lived as animals on earth. And some are called "cryptids," mysterious creatures who may exist in other dimensions, and who seem more like phantoms than real animals when they wander into our world. The sidebar, "Black Dogs and Demon Dogs," describes the huge, fiery-eyed black dogs seen in many locations—sometimes as a death omen.

While ghosts can be scary, most of them never harm people, and many never even interact with the living. They seem to be locked in their own reality. But sometimes hauntings "go bad." Chapter 7, "Nasty Hauntings," examines angry ghosts, **poltergeists**, and demonic spirits that have wreaked havoc. "The Curse of the Bell Witch" sidebar highlights one of America's famous nasty hauntings, the Bell Witch of Adams, Tennessee. Young Besty Bell got the worst of it. Her father died, and some say the angry ghost or spirit caused his death. Finally, what do you do if you want a ghost to leave? The sidebar "Getting Rid of Ghosts" reveals some tried-and-true methods.

Can we ever get proof that ghosts exist? Ever since the camera was invented, people have tried to take pictures of ghosts. Chapter 8, "Ghosts on Camera," reveals that the history of **spirit photography** is full of scandal and fraud. Even a brilliant man like Sir Arthur Conan Doyle, who created Sherlock Holmes, fell for phony fairy photos. Despite all the problems, there are some amazing photographs of ghosts that have never been debunked. Today's ghost hunters are always trying to get better and more convincing photographic evidence of ghosts and spirits. But what about **orbs**, those mysterious balls of light that that everybody seems to get in their shots, especially with digital cameras? Orbs are the subject of a big controversy in the ghost-hunting world, as you will discover in the sidebar, "Orbs: Fake Ghosts or the Real Deal?"

Another major line of research for proof of ghosts is **EVP, or electronic voice phenomena.** Put your audio recorder out, leave it running—and maybe ghosts will leave a message. Chapter 9, "Spirit Voices: Ghosts Who Are Heard but Not Seen," tells all about EVP: how it was discovered, how it works, and what it means. You can even learn how to do EVP yourself from the sidebar, "Do-It-Yourself EVP."

No ghost book would be complete without tips on how to be a ghost hunter. As you will see in Chapter 10, "Ghost Hunting with the Pros," a lot goes into becoming a successful ghost hunter. Find out what you need to know, own, and do in order to become an investigator. The sidebar "Borley Rectory: The Most Investigated Haunted Place in History" describes one approach to a haunted site that ushered in the era of tech, or technological, ghost hunting. Tech has changed a great deal since those days! Don't get so hooked on tech, however, that you overlook the benefits of psychics. The sidebar "Seeing Dead People: The Psychic Side of Ghost Hunting," tells how psychics work, and what they contribute to ghost hunting.

We'll wrap up our adventure into the shadowy world of ghosts with a timeline of events and cases, and a list of resources to consult for more research. Many amateur ghost hunters make valuable contributions to the field. Perhaps you'll be one of them!

Dead People Who Don't Go Away

In the middle of a cold winter night in 1974, the fire department in West Barnstable, Massachusetts, received a distressing alarm. One of the most historic homes in the area, the Barnstable House, was on fire. Built in 1716, the house was located on Old Kings Highway, a vein of road running the length of Cape Cod—and one of the most haunted stretches of highway in North America. The Barnstable House was known as "The House of Eleven Ghosts."

Two fire trucks raced to the home. Firefighters found the large, white-clapboard colonial structure ablaze. Was anyone inside? The house had not been a private residence for many years, but it was now a restaurant. At 3:00 a.m., it was, of course, closed.

Looking up, several firefighters saw a woman standing in one of the upstairs windows. They rushed inside, but when they got to the room, no one was there. In fact, the woman was nowhere inside the burning house.

But down on the ground, other startled firefighters saw her. Clothed in a long white dress, with long blonde hair blowing about her shoulders, she floated about two feet above the snow-covered ground. She looked sad. "Where is the Dalmatian?" she asked. Before anyone could react, she vanished into the smoky air.

No one knows who the ghost is—or what happened to her dog. There was no dog on the premises, and no recent record of a Dalmatian living there. For much of its history the Barnstable House has been the home of ghosts, some of them known and some of them anonymous. One known ghost is Edmund Hawes, an owner who committed suicide over money troubles by hanging himself from a tree in the yard in 1776. Another ghost is a little girl, Lucy. According to legend, she died in the well to the underground stream that runs beneath the house. Her mother is a ghost, too. She sits in a rocking chair inside the house, mournfully waiting for her daughter to come back.

Many people have seen the ghosts of the Barnstable House. Around the world there are thousands of homes and buildings just like it. They are haunted by the ghosts of dead people who don't go away, but linger in a twilight world that belongs half to life and half to death.

What exactly is a ghost? Do ghosts really exist? People have had experiences with ghosts for thousands of years. It might seem that experiences alone prove that ghosts exist. But despite all the testimony, there are skeptics who say ghosts are not real. Getting hard proof of ghosts has so far proven almost impossible. They don't sit for photographs and they don't give interviews. There are photographs, film clips, and audio recordings that some researchers say capture ghosts in action, but these, too, are disputed by skeptics.

WHAT IS A GHOST?

The simplest definition of a ghost is that it is the spirit of a dead person, or animal, for animal ghosts have been reported for as long as human ghosts. Since ancient times, people have believed that ghosts happen when some souls do not travel to the afterlife, but remain attached to the world of the living. Or they somehow find a way to return to this world. Whatever the reason, the presence of a ghost spells trouble in most people's view.

There are different terms for ghosts: phantoms, phantasms, **specters**, the walking dead, **revenants**, and **apparitions**. Some names have fallen in and out of fashion throughout history. For example, the term

Figure 1.1   *Known as "The House of Eleven Ghosts," the Barnstable House has been haunted since it was built in the eighteenth century.*   (Author's collection)

revenant is rarely used today. Apparition applies to phantom experiences of the living as well as the dead. An apparition of a living person involves seeing that person when he or she actually is in a distant location. Bilocation—the ability to be in two places at once—is a possible explanation. Apparitions of the living are the subject of separate research. This book will focus on apparitions of the dead.

Demons, angels, fairies, elementals, and other spirits can haunt a place and act like ghosts, but they are not the same as ghosts.

Inanimate objects can be ghosts, too. There are phantom houses, trains, landscapes, cars, and other things.

Human beings have always believed in an afterlife. Every culture throughout history has formed beliefs about what that afterlife is like, how a soul gets there, and what happens to it there. Some afterlives are happy places and others are not so pleasant. The ancient Greeks thought the afterlife—in Hades, the underworld—to be a drab and dreary place. The souls of the dead, called shades, longed for the color and excitement of life. Under certain circumstances, they were able to leave Hades and return to the world. Most often, the shades, as ghosts, visited the living in their dreams.

Most cultures also have had beliefs about how the dead can return to the world of the living. Whether or not this was a good or bad thing varied from culture to culture. In China, Japan, and other parts of the world, dead ancestors remain part of a person's extended family. Thus, their return can be welcomed. In other cultures the dead are not supposed to return. When they do, it is considered unnatural, even unholy. In Christianity, souls are supposed to go to either heaven or hell for eternity. Some people believe that souls cannot return from the dead, and therefore ghosts are demons in disguise, intended to trick people.

Regardless of whether or not ghosts belong in the living world, they are unpredictable, and that makes them frightening. Not all ghosts behave the same way, but most of them do fall into patterns that have been identified throughout the ages.

THE RESTLESS DEAD

Some ghosts willfully come back to the world of the living. Some seem to be stuck and unable to make the journey to the afterlife. These ghosts haunt places where they died or places that were familiar to them during life. They are intelligent and are able to find ways to communicate with the living. There are many reasons why they are restless.

They had unfinished business when they died, and they are determined to finish it. Unfinished business might be a family matter, a business deal, or revenge of a wrong. Remember the Greeks?

Those ghosts visiting in dreams always came for a purpose, such as to deliver a message, advice, or a warning.

In 1921 James L. Chaffin, a farmer in North Carolina, died. He had written a new will and hid it in a coat pocket before he died. None of his family members knew about it. His existing will left everything to one son instead of dividing it up among his wife and four sons. Four years later one of the sons who had been left out had dreams in which the ghost of his dead father visited him. James told the son about the new will. It was found and was accepted in court. Chaffin's estate was redistributed to all his heirs.

In 1897 a young woman named Elva Zona Hester Shue was found dead in her home near Greenbrier, West Virginia. Her neck was broken, and it was assumed that she fell down the stairs. However, she had been strangled by her husband, Erasmus Stribbling Trout Shue. After Zona (as she was called) was buried, her ghost came to her mother in dreams to expose the murdering husband. Zona's mother succeeded in bringing the man to trial. The ghost's testimony was actually admitted as evidence. Trout Shue was convicted and sent to prison for life. He died in jail in 1900. The Greenbrier Ghost is one of the rare cases where a ghost went to court! Zona's ghost never came back once justice was done.

They died suddenly and do not know they are dead.   According-ing to this belief, if a person dies unexpectedly in an accident, natural disaster, or crime, they may not find their way to the afterlife. Instead, they are stuck in a timeless limbo, usually near the place where they died. Psychics and mediums who can communicate with them may help them to the other side.

They were not buried or were buried improperly.   It is a wide-spread belief that the dead must be properly honored in burial, or, if they are not buried, then in funeral rites. Many ghost stories involve ghosts who return to the living to beg for proper burial or complain

The Top Ten Spookiest Places

Do ghosts like to be in certain places? Maybe so, according to "most haunted" cases recorded through history. Here are the top ten places most likely to be haunted:

1 **Private homes:** Homes collect the emotional energy of people who live and die in them. Also, they may be built on ground with unusual geomagnetic energy.

2 **Castles with dungeons:** The violence, torture, and agonizing deaths of victims imprisoned in dungeons create fertile ground for negative hauntings, which can range from imprints to ugly thought-forms.

3 **Funeral homes:** Sometimes people don't move on right after they die. Instead, they linger around their bodies. Funeral parlors can collect the confused and unhappy energy, which turns into hauntings. Sometimes the dead choose to stay—and they may decide they like the funeral home.

4 **Cemeteries and graveyards:** Imprint ghosts and people who haven't moved on may haunt graves. Spirits attached to certain places in the land haunt the cemeteries that are built on "their" sites.

5 **Battlefields:** Sites of fear, violence, and death on a mass scale send a lot of blood and bones into the soil. Battlefields are often full of imprint reenactments and souls who have not moved on.

6 **Accident scenes:** Sudden death can create imprints that linger where accidents take place. Sometimes souls who don't know they're dead stay on, too.

7 **Hospitals and institutions:** These places are often haunted by both patients who die there and the ghosts of people who tend them—nurses, doctors, and staff.

Figure 1.2 *Hooded figures are said to haunt many graveyards, as suggested by this photograph.* (Fortean Picture Library)

8 **Hotels, inns, and pubs:** Ghosts sometimes like to haunt favorite places, places where something emotional or traumatic happened to them, or places they visited frequently in life.

9 **Crossroads:** Folklore holds that any place where roads or paths intersect are targets for hauntings. Ghosts and spirits get confused at crossroads and become stuck there.

10 **Schools:** Youthful energy seems to make it easy for ghosts of students, faculty, and staff to stay on at their schools.

about the way they were buried. In earlier times the deceased's family and friends washed the body, dressed it, and carried it out of the home and to the graveyards. There are many superstitions about following the proper burial procedures, so that when the dead were placed six feet under, they would stay there.

One of the first ghost stories ever recorded in the Western world was the haunting of Athenodorus, a philosopher who lived in Athens during the first century. Athenodorus was poor, and all he could afford to rent was a house with a horrible reputation for being haunted by the ugly ghost of an old man. The ghost was a chain-clanker. Literally. In fact, this story probably created the stereotype of chain-clanking ghosts. The ghost dragged about the house in his leg chains, moaning and scaring away all tenants.

Finally, having no other choice of places to live, Athenodorus moved in. When the ghost appeared Athenodorus was not afraid as others had been. The ghost led him outside and pointed to a spot on the ground. The next day Athenodorus had the ground dug up there. A human skeleton was found, still shackled to rusted chains. The bones were given a proper burial, and the house was haunted no more.

They committed suicide or a crime and are unhappy. In most cultures suicide is forbidden and carries a heavy penalty. The ghosts of suicides are believed to return and lament their mistakes. Similarly, criminals, especially murderers, are believed to be restless in their graves.

They were cursed before they died. A curse by a witch or sorcerer, or even an angry family member or friend is believed to cause some people to return as ghosts.

They are vampires. In the folklore of certain cultures, especially Eastern Europe, the restless dead are vampires who attack the living for their blood and life force energy. Like the shades of ancient Greece, they are jealous of the living.

IMPRINTS AND RECORDINGS

Many ghosts are not the actual presence of the spirit of a dead person but a record left behind. For reasons unknown, events or personalities are recorded on some invisible medium. When the right person comes along under the right circumstances, the recording plays.

Imprints haunt the places where events occurred. No one knows exactly why imprints are made. Strong emotions seem to be a major factor. Many hauntings concern unhappy or violent events: scenes of murder, suicide, illness, battle, and accident. Any events that involve intense emotion are candidates for hauntings. Few hauntings are of happy emotional scenes, such as weddings. The emotional peaks felt by the living when the events happen may somehow become fixed in unseen space. They replay over and over again.

Imprints usually run out of energy, as though their psychic battery runs down. When that happens, the hauntings grow weaker and weaker, and then stop altogether. Some imprints last for many centuries, while others last only for a few months. Why do some last so long? Reasons may be the intensity of emotion behind the original events, and a concentration of natural earth energy that helps to hold the imprints (an idea we'll explore later).

Most modern ghost investigators believe that most hauntings are imprints.

RECURRING AND ANNIVERSARY GHOSTS

Some ghosts show up only at certain times, such as the anniversary of an event. These are imprint ghosts. They reenact scenes.

President Abraham Lincoln was assassinated in office on April 14, 1865. After his body laid in state in the White House, it was taken by train on a 14-day funeral trip, stopping in various cities. It ended in Springfield, Illinois, where Lincoln was buried. Since then, every April at the anniversary of the assassination, a phantom funeral train travels the tracks along the route taken by the official funeral train. The ghost train is seen and heard—but it never reaches its destination.

URBAN LEGENDS

Some recurring ghosts are imprints based in part on real people and events and urban legends, which are embellished stories that evolve from real events. The stories often involve "true" accounts told to a friend of a friend of a friend.

Among the most famous urban legend ghosts are phantom hitch-hikers who are always seen along the same stretch of road—like Resurrection Mary, discussed in the next chapter. Other examples are ghosts that always ride the same train or sit at the same table in a restaurant, and phantom ships always seen in the same spot, such as where a real ship was sunk or wrecked. The ghosts are tied to real events, but the details of their hauntings have grown over time as stories have been retold.

Some urban legends have no known historical source. The "Hooked Spirit" is a ghost urban legend of Chicago's famous Bachelor's Grove Cemetery, related to a similar story in which the menace is a real person rather than a ghost. The story is as follows: A boy takes a girl on a date to the cemetery, hoping the Hooked Spirit will scare her. This way the boy can be the hero and protect her. Instead, the girl asks to be driven home. Disappointed, the boy agrees. When they arrive at her home, they find a hook hanging on the car door handle, as though an evil ghost had tried to get in.

SHADOW PEOPLE

Some ghosts do not appear as filmy, semi-transparent figures, but as dark, shadowy outlines. Shadow people, as they are called, are found in some haunted places. They usually look like men in shape, and sometimes they wear hats. They may be a type of human ghost. Some

Figure 1.3 *Waverly Hills Sanatorium, where thousands died, is the site of various hauntings and other paranormal phenomena.*
(Author's collection)

ghost researchers think that shadow people are not human ghosts, however, but are beings from other dimensions that are drawn to haunted places.

Waverly Hills Sanatorium, an abandoned tuberculosis hospital in the Louisville, Kentucky, area, is famous for its ghosts and shadow people. Thousands of people died there during tuberculosis epidemics in the 1920s and 1930s. The shadow people are dark forms that are seen moving about the long corridors, which are in ruins.

Now You See 'Em, Now You Don't

On a warm night in April, a group of teens in Victoria, British Columbia, decide it would be fun to go out ghost hunting. They want to see for themselves if it's true that the ghost of Doris Gravlin, the most famous ghost in Victoria, really haunts the Victoria Golf Course. They get more than they bargained for.

The wide-open spaces of the deserted fairways look strange and foreboding in the darkness. The boys and girls urge each other on with dares in hushed voices and muffled laughter. The golf course runs alongside the cold waters of Oakland Bay. They make their way to the point where Gravlin's body was found tangled in weeds on the shoreline near the seventh tee. The water glistens with a supernatural look.

Everything is still and quiet. There is no ghost. It looks like the night's ghost hunt is a bust.

Disappointed but also relieved, the teens relax and joke around. Then one of the girls shrieks and points into the darkness. Rushing toward them at unearthly speed is the unmistakable apparition of a young woman wearing a white dress. Her face is twisted in a look of horror, and her arms are reaching out as though she wants to grab whoever sees her. Coming with her is a terribly cold wind.

Screaming, the kids scatter in terror. But almost as soon as the ghost is seen, it disappears.

When they calm down the teens sort out what happened. Two members of the group saw nothing but got scared when others started to scream and run. Several saw the ghost but were not certain what they saw. And several were convinced that they had indeed seen and met the famous Doris Gravlin.

Gravlin's ghost has appeared to many people since she was found murdered on the golf course in 1936. She seems especially fond of teens, and local folklore holds that if couples see her ghost, it's an omen that they will not marry. In fact, her ghost sometimes wears a white wedding dress, even though she was wearing ordinary clothing the night she met her doom.

Gravlin was an ordinary young woman who was miserable in an unhappy marriage. After being separated from her husband, Victor, she agreed to meet him one night at the Oakland Bay Beach Hotel near the golf course. They went out for a walk on the golf course. She thought they were going to make up and get back together. Instead, she was murdered and her body tossed off the golf course point.

Victor disappeared the same night. His murdered body was found nearly two months later near the ninth tee. The crimes were never solved. Doris is the only one of the tragic pair to remain at the scene of their last night on earth.

Gravlin's ghost is like many that haunt the places of violence and unhappiness. She appears suddenly, can be seen by multiple witnesses at the same time, and then disappears just as suddenly. Sometimes Gravlin's ghost even manages to grab hold of a witness for a fleeting moment.

Everyone who goes looking for ghosts hopes that they will see one. The truth is ghosts are very elusive. Phantoms like Gravlin are the exception rather than the rule. Most ghosts are heard, smelled, and felt—but seldom seen!

To make matters more complicated, ghosts are not experienced equally by all people. Just like the teens described above, not everyone who is present when a ghost makes itself known will see, hear, smell, or feel the same things. Some people experience nothing at all. The unevenness of experience leads to disagreements about whether or not ghosts are real. However, many witnesses have had experiences that have convinced them that ghosts do exist.

SENSING GHOSTS

If you are near ghosts, your first clues are most likely to be physical. Your skin tingles or crawls, or the hair on the back of your neck and on your arms stands up. These are age-old, primitive responses alerting us to the unseen presence of potential danger. While most ghosts are not dangerous, most are unseen, and their invisible presence may change the atmosphere of a place and trigger our automatic body responses.

You may also feel a strange tightening or unpleasant sensation in the gut. Or, you may have a generalized, overall feeling that "something" you can't see is present. There may be a ringing or buzzing noise in your ears. Persons who have developed their psychic ability may also get mental impressions of the ghost along with the physical sensations. They may "see" the ghost in their mind's eye. (The psychic sensing of ghosts will be discussed further later in the book.)

Ghosts often are accompanied by cold spots and breezes. When a ghost is nearby, suddenly the temperature plunges, or there is one spot in a room that is unnaturally and inexplicably cold.

HEARING GHOSTS

Ghosts seem fond of being heard and not seen. You may hear all kinds of noises that you cannot explain: footsteps, movements of objects, breaking of objects, animal sounds, battle sounds, and music. You may even hear the sounds of events that took place in the past. During World War II a fierce air and sea battle took place near Dieppe, France, on August 19, 1942. The ghostly sounds of shellfire, dive-bombing airplanes, and soldiers shouting are still heard there, especially on the anniversary of the battle.

Resurrection Mary Keeps Trying to Go Home

She was a pretty blue-eyed blonde, an ideal date, and she loved to dance. But one fateful night, she changed from Mary, teenage sweetheart, to Resurrection Mary, a ghost doomed to hitchhike home over and over again. Only "home" isn't a house—it's a cemetery!

Resurrection Mary is one of Chicago's most famous ghosts. She has been seen frequently since 1936, either at the Willowbrook Ballroom, where she had her final date, or walking along the road where she is said to have died after being struck by a hit-and-run driver.

The story goes that Mary, dressed in a fancy white dress and white shoes, went dancing one night at the ballroom, which then was known as the O. Henry Ballroom. She argued with her date and left the ballroom in a huff, walking up Archer Avenue. It's not known how the accident happened—or who was at fault—but Mary was struck and killed by a car. The driver left the scene and was never identified. Mary's heartbroken parents had her buried at Resurrection Cemetery, wearing the white dress and shoes she wore on the last night of her life.

One common sound associated with ghosts is the movement of heavy objects or furniture. You may hear noises like someone dragging heavy furniture across a floor, but no one is there, and nothing is out of place.

Phantom music also is also common, especially if the ghosts were piano players or other types of musicians in life.

SMELLING GHOSTS

Ghosts sometimes make themselves known by sudden smells. Perfumes and tobacco smells favored by the living are trademark identities of their ghosts. Dolley Madison, the wife of James Madison, the third president of the United States, was famous for her lilac perfume,

No one knows who the real Mary was. She has been said to be Anna Marija (Mary) Norkus, a 12-year-old blonde Lithuanian girl who went to the O. Henry in July 1927 to celebrate her birthday. On her way home, the car in which she was riding fell into a ditch and she was killed. But Marija was buried at another cemetery.

Nonetheless, the ghost of Resurrection Mary is real to those who meet her. She is most often seen in winter, especially around Christmastime. She looks very much alive, dressed in her fancy white dress and shoes, and a little shawl too thin for the cold winter night. She flags down cars and asks for a ride, directing the driver to go down Archer Avenue past Resurrection Cemetery. Just as the car nears the cemetery, Mary mysteriously vanishes. Sometimes she asks the driver to stop. Then she gets out, walks through the narrow iron bars of the locked cemetery gates, and disappears.

Resurrection Mary may be more fiction than fact—a "phantom hitchhiker" haunting called an "urban legend," because the story grows over time. But even though the story of her life and death can't be verified, many startled witnesses will testify that her ghost is very real.

and so is her ghost, which haunts their former residence in Washington, D.C.

The Birdcage Theater in Tombstone, Arizona, was one of the most famous saloons in the days of the Wild West. Strong smells of whiskey and tobacco appear suddenly, along with the phantom sounds of gambling, drinking, shouting, singing, and dancing.

SEEING GHOSTS

Only a small number of ghosts are seen, but when they are, the experience can be quite unnerving. Most apparitions are filmy gray or white and are transparent or semi-transparent. Usually they are seen for a split second. You may not see the full figure, but only part of it, such as the upper body or lower body.

Some ghosts appear to be solid and are mistaken for living people. These sightings last longer than those of transparent figures. Thornewood Castle is a large manor home near Tacoma, Washington. It was used as the setting for the television miniseries *Rose Red*, written by Stephen King, about the horrors of a haunted house. The builder of Thornewood, Chester Thorne, is seen about the grounds and house, dressed in his favorite brown suit and riding boots, and as solid in appearance as a living person.

Similarly, the life-like ghost of William N. Chancellor haunts the Blennerhassett Hotel in Parkersburg, West Virginia. Chancellor, the

Figure 2.1 *The ghost of Chester Thorne is sometimes seen on the grounds of Thornewood Castle.* (Author's collection)

mayor of Parkersburg, built the place in 1889 as a private residence. His ghost likes to visit the hotel's library, trailing the smell of his favorite pipe tobacco.

Many sightings of ghosts happen so fast that you're not sure you saw anything strange at all. They flicker briefly in your peripheral vision, but as soon as you turn your head, nothing is there.

OTHER WAYS TO EXPERIENCE GHOSTS

Ghosts have many ways to make their presence known. They have effects on electrical and electromagnetic equipment. Lights turn on and off by themselves. Appliances spring to life on their own, turn off on their own, or malfunction. Ghost investigators are all too familiar with fresh batteries going dead in cameras and recorders and equipment not working properly.

A ghost at the Judge's Bench, a restaurant and tavern in Ellicott City, Maryland, likes to flush the toilet in the ladies' room, startling customers.

Ghosts also are associated with the movements and disappearances of objects. People who live in or visit haunted places find that small objects are moved from one location to another without explanation. Or the objects disappear for a while and then reappear in another, often odd, location.

Sometimes, things are rearranged. Pictures mysteriously and repeatedly are found fallen from walls, candles never stay in their holders, curtains and blinds never stay closed. At the Stephen Daniels House, a bed-and-breakfast in Salem, Massachusetts, that dates to the eighteenth century, a ghost likes to carefully raise a drawn window blind during the night in one of the guestrooms.

Why are there so many variations in the way people experience ghosts? The study of ghosts would be much easier if people had consistent experiences that could be measured and compared.

Perhaps one of the reasons why ghosts are so unpredictable is that they don't come from the same source and are not created in the same way. In fact, scientific research points us in that direction: all ghosts are not created equally. The *consciousness* of the living and the energy from electromagnetic and geomagnetic sources seem to influence the how and why of ghosts.

Where Do Ghosts Come From?

It may seem obvious that ghosts come from the afterlife. Up until the nineteenth century, that explanation satisfied most people. In the nineteenth century scientists began to study the paranormal and to look for evidence proving that there is indeed survival after death. Since then, many explanations for ghosts have been put forward. Some of them might surprise you.

Even though people around the world have experienced ghosts since ancient times, science does not accept ghosts as proof of an afterlife. Ghost experiences are anecdotal—stories—and are not hard evidence. For scientific proof, there must be reliable, measurable data.

Survival after death and the existence of the afterlife are beliefs held by many people. These types of beliefs are called articles of faith, that is, we believe them even without scientific proof. These beliefs are shaped by our religious, spiritual, and cultural environments.

The nineteenth century ushered in exciting changes in Western society concerning beliefs about the paranormal and survival. One major movement was Spiritualism, a new religion that focused on communication with spirits as proof of the afterlife. The start of Spiritualism in 1848 is credited to the Fox sisters: Maggie, Kate, and Leah. The Fox sisters lived in Hydesville, New York. Maggie and Kate discovered, by accident, that they could communicate with a spirit in their house by interpreting rapping sounds supposedly made by the spirit.

Spiritualism became the rage on both sides of the Atlantic. Mediums everywhere held **séances** to communicate with the dead. People were fascinated, and scientists were intrigued.

In 1882 a group of scholars and scientists came together in London and founded the Society for Psychical Research (SPR). Their purpose was to attract the brightest and best minds to bring science and religion together by finding scientific evidence to prove Spiritualist and paranormal phenomena. The SPR was followed by the founding of the American Society for Psychical Research (ASPR) in 1886 in New York City.

Members of the SPR, ASPR, and similar groups studied mediums, apparitions, telepathy, mesmerism (the early name for hypnotism), and

Figure 3.1 *Members of a group called "Questors" perform a séance inside the Manila Film Center to drive away spirits that are believed to be still holed up inside the building.* (Pat Roque/AP)

other phenomena. The SPR collected 5,700 reports of apparitions of both the living and the dead. In 1889 they conducted a Census of Hallucinations, which drew 17,000 replies. Nearly 10 percent of the people who answered said they had experienced an apparition of either the living or the dead.

More census surveys were conducted in America, France, and Germany. The results were the same. Roughly 10 percent of the adult population claimed to have experienced an apparition. The percentage held true for a repeat census taken by the SPR in Britain in 1988.

In more recent times, the percentages have increased dramatically. Believers in ghosts in America alone jumped to 27 percent in 1973, 42 percent in 1987, and 51 percent in 2003. Studies also show that the younger you are, the more likely you are to be a believer.

Are more people converting from skepticism to belief, or are more people just willing to admit their belief? The answer probably lies somewhere in between. The increasing media popularity of ghosts and hauntings has made the paranormal more acceptable to a mainstream audience.

Both scientists and amateur ghost investigators have put forward ideas explaining the how and why of ghosts. Just as there are different types of ghosts, there are different explanations that fit some ghosts and not others. Let's look at the most significant ones.

PORTALS

The idea that ghosts slip through portals between worlds may sound new, but it's actually quite old. The ancients believed that at certain times of the year, the veil between the worlds of the living and the dead was thin, and the dead could easily come into our world for a brief time. When they did so, they were dangerous and troublesome to the living.

Halloween is the modern version of one of these ancient thin-veil times. In earlier times people dressed in disguises to trick the ghosts so that the ghosts would not bother them. This became the modern custom of trick-or-treating.

Many modern ghost hunters think that certain haunted places are located where portals between dimensions exist. The ghosts are the dead who exist in the afterlife, and they have pathways and openings to re-enter our world.

RECORDINGS

In Chapter 1 we discussed imprint ghosts and recurring ghosts. Somehow impressions of people, animals, events, and buildings remain energized and act like a cosmic DVD or CD on continuous play. Intense emotions often are involved in the events. Feelings and thoughts seem to leave a permanent record.

An explanation for this can be found in Eastern mystical philosophy. The *akasha*, a Sanskrit term for sky, is an invisible life-force substance that exists everywhere in creation. It holds the records of everything that has ever been thought, felt, and done. The Akashic Records are a giant library of everything that has happened in history.

Early psychical researchers adopted the idea of the *akasha*, calling it "psychic ether." Normally, we do not have access to the Akashic Records. Ghosts and hauntings may be playbacks from the records that bleed into our dimension.

PIECES OF SOUL OR PERSONALITY

In Chapter 1, we discussed trapped souls, who may not make the transition to the afterlife, and thus appear to us as ghosts. A related explanation for ghosts is that after death, a piece of soul or personality—or essence—is left behind. It is like a shell, only partially animated.

Versions of this explanation have been shared by different cultures around the planet. The ancient Egyptians believed that after death, the soul split into two. The *ba* was related to the individual and the body, while the *ka* was more a part of group consciousness. In Chinese thought the soul splits into two or three parts after death. In Melanesian thought the soul splits into good and bad ghosts, each of which has its own afterlife.

TELEPATHY

Telepathy, which in this case means thought transfer between the living and the dead, was a favored theory of some early psychical researchers as an explanation for ghosts. Two founders of SPR, Edmund Gurney and Frederic W.H. Myers, believed that ghosts are created when the dead telepathically contact the living. The ghost is created by the living as a vehicle for contact.

Other psychical researchers also have liked the idea that ghosts spring out of the minds of the living. Some have proposed that ghosts are hallucinations produced by telepathy among the living. Ghosts witnessed by more than one person at the same time would be a type of collective telepathy springing up in all the minds at the same time. Some, like parapsychologist Tony Cornell of Cambridge, England, who has spent 50 years investigating paranormal phenomena, say that all psychical phenomena, including ghosts, poltergeists, séance-room phenomena, and so on, are completely created within the mind. No one, however, has explained how the human mind might produce all of these effects under all conditions.

THOUGHT-FORMS

This theory holds that at least some ghosts are not dead people, but are artificial forms like fantasies or dreams that are created by collective thought and emotion. An example is the terrible haunting at Castle Leap in Ireland. The castle, now in ruins, had a dungeon with spikes on the floor. Victims were thrown into the dungeon and were impaled

Are Ghosts Just in Your Head?

It's no accident that tales of hauntings are often set on dark and stormy nights. According to science, that's when the brain is most likely to experience ghosts and poltergeists. In fact, a whole host of factors are involved in hauntings—independent of the ghosts themselves!

Skeptics are fond of saying that ghosts are all in your head, that they're the products of an overactive imagination. In part, they're right. What goes on in your head affects whether or not you have a paranormal experience and the kind of experience you have. Also important is the level of geomagnetic activity in your physical location.

For decades neuroscientists have been studying how the brain works when people have mystical and paranormal experiences. One of the leading researchers in the world is Michael Persinger, a professor and clinical psychologist at Laurentian University in Sudbury, Ontario, Canada. Persinger has shown that mystical and paranormal experiences can be created by stimulating certain parts of the brain with low-intensity electromagnetic waves. To do this he puts his subjects in a room where they are deprived them of light and sound; the isolation quiets the nerve cells that are involved in seeing and hearing. Then he places a helmet on their heads that creates a magnetic field pattern over the right hemisphere of the brain.

Persinger and others also have shown that geomagnetic energy has an effect on the brain. The main part of the Earth's geomagnetic field is like a huge bar magnet that runs through the center of the planet.

on the spikes. They were left to die slow and agonizing deaths. Those who missed the spikes were left to starve to death.

Castle Leap is haunted by a horrid, animalistic form that some believe is a thought-form created by the human suffering of the dungeon victims. Their agonized thoughts and feelings collected together and were somehow able to become a ghostly life form.

Every day there are regular, small changes in the strength of the field. Stronger and more irregular changes are affected by activity on the sun, and by the Earth's relation to other planets in the solar system. Sunspot activity and solar flares can cause huge fluctuations in the geomagnetic field.

Magnetically stormy days and nights are the times when reports of ghosts and poltergeists increase. This indicates that something in the brain may react to geomagnetic fluctuations. In paranormal terms, doorways to the unseen swing open.

Other research has shown that places on the Earth that have natural and unusually high and fluctuating geomagnetic fields often are associated with a wide range of paranormal experiences. For example, many sacred sites, such as Stonehenge, certain mountains, healing springs, and so forth, seem to have a mysterious power. Visitors to such places report encounters with extraterrestrials, angels, strange lights, odd creatures, spirits, and of course, ghosts.

Using high-tech equipment, ghost investigators and scientists have found that some sites famous for their haunting activity sit on places high in unusual and fluctuating geomagnetic energy. This does not mean that the energy creates ghosts, but only that it is associated with ghosts and other phenomena.

Are the skeptics right? Are ghosts all in the head, the result of the brain reacting to electromagnetic and geomagnetic energy? On the contrary, the research shows that we have the hard wiring necessary to have paranormal experiences. Otherwise, we'd never know what's out there.

TIME SLIPS

Perhaps some hauntings are not in our real time. Instead, we may briefly slip into the past. How much we slip determines the details of our ghost experience. Retrocognition, the ability to see into the past, is a term used in **psychical research** for this type of experience.

The most famous ghost experience thought to be a time slip is the Versailles Ghost case. In August 1901 two English academics, Eleanor Jourdain and Annie Moberly, visited the Versailles Palace in France. They strolled about the grounds and visited the Petite Trianon. This smaller house on the grounds was built by King Louis XV in the 1770s. His grandson and successor, Louis XVI, gave it to his wife, Marie Antoinette. Marie loved to spend time there in the lush days before the French Revolution. When the revolution came and the monarchy was destroyed, both Louis XVI and Marie Antoinette were executed by beheading.

During their visit Jourdain and Moberly saw numerous people in period costumes dating to the time of the French Revolution. They assumed that the people were part of the staff who were dressed for

Figure 3.2 *The Palace of Versaille near Paris, France, where visitors have reported strange encounters.* (Hugh Rooney; Eye Ubiquitous/Corbis)

effect. Then they were startled to see some of the costumed people vanish. Both women felt weird while they were there.

Later the women were able to describe seeing buildings as they had looked in the past. Both of them concluded that they had experienced a time slip to 1789, and they had actually seen Marie Antoinette herself, sitting in the Petite Trianon garden.

In later years other people reported similar experiences at Versailles. Psychical researchers studied their reports, but no satisfactory explanations have ever been given to either support the time slip explanation or disprove it.

CURSES

In magic and sorcery a curse is a spell that is intended to harm or kill. A curse also is punishment for wrongdoing.

In folklore the strongest of all curses are the ones uttered by dying people on their deathbeds. Such curses are made with great anger and emotion, which gives them even more power. A dying person might seek to avenge a wrong and utter a curse that another person will never rest in peace. If the curse works, the cursed person will haunt as a ghost, trapped after death by the curse.

The Flying Dutchman is a phantom sailing ship cursed to sail forever around the Cape of Good Hope, the southern tip of Africa. The ship's dead crew and captain are ghosts on board. The ship is an omen of disaster in bad weather.

The Flying Dutchman may be based in part on real events, for the African cape was famous for sinking ships in its dangerous currents. Over time, the legend of the doomed crew and ship developed in storytelling. According to one version the ship was sailing around the cape when bad weather arose. The crew begged to head for safe harbor. The captain refused and challenged God to sink the ship. Instantly an apparition appeared and cursed the captain to sail forever and to torment his crew.

DO WE REALLY KNOW?

The above explanations for ghosts are plausible. But even after centuries of thinking about ghosts and studying them, we still do not know for certain why ghosts exist, and why they behave in the ways they do. Perhaps we have yet to discover other explanations for ghosts.

Screaming Banshees
and Death Omen Ghosts

One of the most feared apparitions is the death omen ghost, a special type of spirit that haunts families and places. According to folklore to see one of these terrible forms almost always spells bad luck—even death.

Death omen ghosts exist all over the world. You may have heard of the most famous one, the banshee, a Gaelic name for a specter found in Ireland, Scotland, throughout the British Isles, and also in America, where immigrants brought their Old World supernatural beliefs.

In the 1800s in West Virginia, a banshee haunted a prominent family. Thomas Marr was a Scotsman who decided to go to America to make a better life for himself. In 1836 he arrived in West Virginia, where he founded a town that was named after him: Marrtown. Marr married a local woman, Mary, and they established a prosperous farm. Their happy life was ruined by the Civil War (1861–65), which brought financial hardship and loss to many. There was scarcely a family not affected by the war.

To make ends meet Marr got a job as a night watchman on a bridge near Marrtown. Every night he rode out on his horse to the bridge. He stood watch in the cold and often in miserable weather. It was dark and lonely, and the woods seemed full of mysterious life.

On several occasions Marr caught sight of a stranger on horseback as he traveled to and from work. The figure was huddled beneath a hooded shroud. Marr could not tell if it was a man or a woman. Whenever he rode closer both horse and rider abruptly vanished.

Marr told Mary about the rider. Neither one of them realized the awful truth: the figure was not a living person but a banshee come to foretell Marr's death.

On February 5, 1876, Marr went to work at the bridge. He did not come back at his usual time. As the hours passed Mary grew more and more worried. When she heard a horse approach the farmhouse, she thought that her beloved husband was home at last. But instead she was greeted by a horrible sight. A shrouded figure whose face remained hidden sat atop a horse that looked supernatural. The figure spoke in a chilling voice, announcing that Thomas Marr was dead. As Mary stood in shock, the horse and rider vanished.

True to the spirit's message, Marr was found dead. How he died is not known. He may have had a heart attack or a stroke. Or perhaps he was frightened to death by the banshee itself.

When Mary died many years later at age 90, the banshee appeared again, but only as a woman's voice that shrieked and cried as Mary's corpse was laid out in her house. The sounds of rattling chains came from the attic.

Banshees are not always the ghosts of the human dead, but a special type of haunting spirit. They appear as females. Sometimes they are beautiful, and sometimes they are ugly and hideous. In Irish folklore they especially haunt families whose names begin with "Mac" and "O." They appear only when a family member is about to die. They announce the coming death by singing, crying, or shrieking. The sounds are chilling and unpleasant. Whoever hears them knows beyond doubt what they mean. Once a banshee appears, there is no avoiding fate.

Banshees have long, flowing yellow hair and wear long dresses, cloaks, or shrouds that are all white, all red, all gray, or all black. When they are ugly, their hair is stringy and messy, and their clothing is tattered.

Banshees appear outside homes and also may be seen in places in nature. The Bean-Nigh, also known as Little-Washer-By-the-Ford, is a type of banshee who appears by the side of a stream. She washes the bloodstained clothing of the person who is about to die. She is said to be the ghost of a woman who died in childbirth. She is small and ugly, and is usually dressed in green.

Like the one attached to Thomas Marr, many banshees ride ghostly horses. Some fly through the air at night, silhouetted against the moon, crying mournfully.

Figure 4.1 *Artist's rendering of a banshee.* (Fortean Picture Library)

Immigrants like Thomas Marr brought banshee and other supernatural beliefs to North America. Banshee lore is especially strong in Appalachian Mountains communities and in areas where many Irish and Scottish settlers made their homes.

There are many other types of death omen ghosts. Phantom coaches, carts, cars, trains, ships, and other vehicles that come to take away the souls of the dead are common in folklore. Variations of them arise in local areas. Death may be soon or months away, but it is certain within a year of certain sightings.

The horse-drawn death coach is a common death omen ghost. It usually is a black coach drawn by black horses, driven by a man dressed all in black. Sometimes the horses are headless, and sometimes the driver is headless. The coach appears at a house where someone is about to die.

The Coach-A-Bower of Mineral Wells and Elizabeth, West Virginia, is a black hearse with a coffin strapped on top, drawn by two white headless horses. Coach-A-Bower is derived from the original Gaelic name, Coiste-Bodhar.

A modern version of the Coach-A-Bower seen in West Virginia is a black automobile hearse with velvet curtains that are pulled shut. The vehicle dates to the 1950s and is seen driving along Route 14.

GHOSTS OF PEOPLE

Persons who have met violent or unhappy ends sometimes haunt places or families as death omen ghosts. The "radiant boy" is such a ghost who appears in the folklore of England and Europe. A radiant boy is a glowing ghost of a boy murdered by his mother. Sometimes the radiant boy forecasts death and other times bad luck.

The ghost of William Darrell haunts Littlecote House, a stately manor home in Wiltshire, England. Darrell lived in the sixteenth century in Littlecote, his family home. A cruel man, he is said to have tossed one of his illegitimate children into a fire. In 1589 he died in a hunting accident when his horse threw him and he broke his neck. Darrell's ghost is a death omen, appearing at Littlecote with a phantom coach and horses whenever a family heir is about to die.

GHOST ANIMALS

Some animal ghosts are indicators of impending death. Black birds and night birds, such as ravens, crows, rooks, and owls, are associated with death. Sometimes an unusual gathering of living black birds is taken as a sign of someone's passing.

Ghostly black dogs are often death omens (see the sidebar on "Black Dogs and Demon Dogs" in Chapter 5.) In mythology dogs are guardians of the dead. Like birds, living dogs and other animals can also forecast death under the right circumstances. A dog that howls at night may be such a sign. In certain areas if the first lamb born on a farm is black, it is a sign that someone in the household will die within a year.

Families and family homes can have their own individual death omens. For example, Arundel Castle, the ancestral home of the dukes of Norfolk in Sussex, England, has its own bird death omen. A white ghost bird flutters against the window to warn of family deaths.

Andrew Lang, a Scotsman who researched the paranormal in the nineteenth and early twentieth centuries, saw his family's death omen a few months before he died of a heart attack. It was a ghostly monster cat.

MYSTERIOUS LIGHTS

Corpse candles and corpse lights are mysterious lights that appear outdoors. The lights are in the shape of white, blue, and yellow balls or candle flames. They bob and float over the ground. They also are called fetch candles, fetch lights, *ignis fatuus*, and even the jack-o-lantern. Lore about them is strong in the British Isles, especially in marshy areas. One possible explanation for the eerie lights is that they are balls of glowing marsh gas. Nonetheless, there are many beliefs about corpse candles as messengers of doom.

Figure 4.2 *Corpse candles are seen as bad omens, sometimes even harbingers of death.* (Fortean Picture Library)

Corpse candles stop and hover at the home of someone who is about to die. Others will stop halfway between the doomed person's home and his ultimate gravesite. Some will even hover over the chest of a sick person in bed. Corpse candles also bounce along seashores and stop at the boats of fishermen who will soon drown.

The *ignis fatuus* (Latin for "foolish fire") covers a wide variety of ghostly lights, some of them death omens. They are said to be the souls of unbaptized children, doomed to wander the earth. In German lore the lights are called *irrlicht*, and they follow funeral processions. In England the Will-o-the-Wisp is an evil light that appears at night and likes to lead travelers astray.

The jack-o-lantern is most often associated with Halloween and trick-or-treating. But in folklore it is the light of a doomed soul who cannot enter either heaven or hell and wanders about, like the unbaptized children. Like the Will-o-the-Wisp, the jack-o-lantern likes to get people lost. Sometimes it is a death omen.

WRAITHS AND DOUBLES

A wraith is a double of a person who has just died or who is about to die. The wraith looks exactly like the living, down to the details of their clothing. It is seen at a distance, often impossibly far away from the actual location of the living person. The wraith may look life-like and real or ghostly and filmy. Those who see it soon learn that the person has died.

Wraiths are also called doppelgangers, fetches, co-walkers, and other names. "Doppelganger" is a German term for "double-goer." Not all appearances of doubles are death omens. They may also be out-of-body projections. In folklore, however, to see a person's double bodes ill.

On rare occasion a person who is about to die sees his own wraith. The poet Percy Bysshe Shelley was said to have seen his own double shortly before he drowned. An undated case from England tells of a

Sir William Napier who checked into a tavern while traveling. He was shocked to see a corpse on the bed in his room, and even more shocked to see that the corpse was himself! The vision vanished, but Napier died soon thereafter.[1]

Figure 4.3 *Though today it is seen as a symbol of the fun of Halloween, in folk-lore a jack-o-lantern is a trapped soul that leads travelers astray and is sometimes a death omen.* (Lorthios/photocuisine/Corbis)

Battles That Never End

In 685 AD, one of the worst battles of the Dark Ages in Britain was fought near Nechanesmere, Scotland. The land was under invasion by the Northumbrians. The battle did not go well for the defending Picts. Most of them were slaughtered, along with their king, Brude mac Beli, and his entire royal bodyguard. The few survivors fled. Behind them they left a landscape littered with the dead, the moaning dying, and the screaming wounded. There were no guns in those days. Soldiers were hacked to death with swords and knives, shot with arrows, and smashed with spiked maces. Dying often took a long and agonizing time. Burying the dead took even longer.

Fast forward to the present times. The countryside around Nechanesmere is lonely and brooding at night. If you pass through at the right time on the right night, the darkness seethes with the ghosts of the battle. Phantoms dressed in seventh-century clothing and carrying phantom torches move about the land, searching for something.

They are the ghosts of the survivors: villagers moving through the blood-soaked battlefield, searching for the wounded, robbing the dying and the dead. They do it over and over again, caught in an eternal twilight zone. For the ghosts, their emotional pain will never end.

Of all events in history, battles fought in wars rank among the most traumatic. Battles are concentrated periods of mass killing. They are filled with emotions, pain, and death. The suffering they cause extends far beyond the battlefields themselves. Lives, families, communities, and even nations are ripped apart.

No wonder that entire battles become ghosts!

There is no certain explanation why battles continue in phantom form. Paranormal researchers believe that the intensity of the emotional pain, physical pain, and violent death—especially on a large scale—leaves a powerful imprint in psychic space, an invisible realm around us. The battles end in real time, but continue and repeat in the invisible realm. A haunting occurs when people are able to experience this invisible realm, even if briefly.

Some researchers also think that some of the souls of dead soldiers become stuck, or earthbound. They linger at the place where they died, not knowing where to go or even how much time passes by.

Nechanesmere is one of the oldest battles known to continue in ghostly form. There are many documented battle ghosts, especially from long wars.

In England a terrible civil war was fought from 1642 to 1651. The war was actually a series of three conflicts, which revolved around the authority of the monarchy versus the authority of Parliament. The Parliamentarians finally won, and the monarchy was replaced with a republican commonwealth government. The war marked a turning point for the destiny of a nation. The impact of it remains in the collective memory of its people and is written in the psychic landscape.

Battles were fought in England, Scotland, and Ireland. The ghosts of those battles are still present. One of those battles was Edgehill, the first major fight of the war. Not only are its ghosts on the land, but they are also in the sky.

The battle of Edgehill was fought on October 23, 1642. The royalist forces of King Charles I opposed the Parliamentary forces of the Earl of Essex. Who won? Opinions are divided. The battle was seen as either a loss for the king or indecisive.

By Christmas Eve the battlefield had been cleared of bodies and wreckage. Most of the bodies had been buried in a graveyard near the battlefield. Shepherds were once again guarding their sheep at night. But this night proved to be quite extraordinary. First the shepherds heard a distant drumming—the sounds of an army approaching. The drumming grew louder and louder. It was joined by phantom shouts and cries, the groaning of wounded and dying men, the metallic clash of weapons, and the screams of wounded and dying horses.

The shepherds then witnessed a huge reenactment of the battle played out by ghost soldiers and horses in the sky. The scene went on for hours, disappearing by dawn.

The next day the amazed shepherds reported what they had seen to the local priest and justice of the peace. The authorities were skeptical. The following night they, the shepherds, and a group of people went out to the battlefield, where they saw and heard exactly the same thing.

The battle repeated two more nights, growing in intensity. Then it repeated every weekend.

Hearing about this wonder, King Charles I sent some of his trusted men to investigate. They, too, saw the phantom battle in the sky. They even recognized some of the dead soldiers. Why was the ghostly battle happening? Witnesses believed that it was caused by the restless spirits of the slain solders, rising up out of their graves nearby.

The weekly sky-theater reenactment of the battle went on for some time and then began decreasing in frequency. It especially appeared on the anniversary of the battle. Even today witnesses see fragments of the battle and occasionally hear sounds. The battlefield and graveyard are described as having a "disturbed" feeling.

America had its own civil war that tore apart the country, less than 100 years after gaining independence from the British. Slavery was at the center of the conflict, along with the economic, political, and social factors affected by slavery. The war started when states in the South seceded and formed the Confederacy to preserve a slave-dependent way of life. The North, the Union, fought against slavery and the secession.

Fought from 1861 to 1865, the Civil War left deep wounds in America—many of them psychic. Wherever battles were fought, ghosts were left behind.

The war took 620,000 lives, more than all the Americans who died in all wars since then combined. The conflict brought the hell of war home in a brutal way. It was the first war to be extensively recorded in graphic photographs. Many diaries and accounts of the battles were written.

One of the bloodiest battles took place at Antietam Creek near Sharpsburg, Maryland, on September 17, 1862. It was a stalemate, though it did not go well for the North. More people died in that one day of fighting than on any other day during the entire war. Estimates are 3,754 dead, 17,292 wounded, and 1,763 missing.

Many of the dead met their end in a single place—Bloody Lane. The lane was actually a sunken road in the earth where Union soldiers were easily picked off. Today Bloody Lane gives off a feeling of dread to the many visitors who come to the site. Phantom cries of battle are heard. At Burnside Bridge where many dead were buried, there are still sounds of phantom drums. Strange blue lights are seen at night. They are believed to be the ghost campfires of ghost soldiers.

Similar hauntings occur at other Civil War battlefields, but none surpass Gettysburg, Pennsylvania, in activity. Gettysburg is probably one of the most haunted battle sites in the world.

Gettysburg, fought July 1–3, 1863, marked the turning point of the Civil War. Prior to that battle the South had the edge over the North. At Gettysburg the North won a decisive victory, gaining an upper hand that lasted until the surrender of the South nearly two years later.

Approximately 165,000 men fought, and there were 50,000 casualties—more than the residents of the entire town of Gettysburg.

Figure 5.1 *A sunken road called "Bloody Lane" crosses the Antietam National Battlefield, site of the bloodiest battle in the American Civil War. Since the battle, it has been a site of haunting activity.* (Lee Snider/Photo Images/Corbis)

Even today Gettysburg has only around 7,000–8,000 residents. The battle is especially known for Pickett's Charge, named after General George Pickett, one of the commanders who led an assault of 12,000 Confederate troops across a huge, open expanse of ground. The Union troops, hidden behind a ridge, shot them to pieces with ease. It was a massacre.

For three days the armies shifted in brutal fighting across land filled with rocks and small hills. In places where intense fighting occurred, there were so many bodies that soldiers could scarcely walk and touch ground. Instead, they walked across corpses. Blood drenched the rocks and the soil.

Amazingly only one civilian was killed, even though the town was filled with gunfire. Jenny Wade, a young woman, was baking bread in

Figure 5.2 *A portion of Gettysburg Battlefield known as Devil's Den.* (Carolyn Kaster/AP)

the kitchen of her sister's home when a bullet tore through the wall and pierced her in the heart. She died instantly. The house, now a museum, is haunted, though opinions are divided as to whether Jenny herself is still there.

Once the fighting was over, the residents of Gettysburg were overwhelmed with tending the wounded, burying the dead, and disposing of the 5,000 dead horses spread over the landscape. Homes, schools, and farms were turned into hospitals. Bullets often shattered bones, and surgeons had no choice but to amputate limbs. Severed hands, feet, arms and legs lay in rotting piles everywhere.

If you can imagine the intensity of this horror, then it comes as no surprise that of all Civil War battlefields, Gettysburg is the most haunted. More than 1 million visitors flock to the battlefield every year. Many come for history, and many come for the ghosts.

Almost anywhere you wander on the enormous battlefield, ghosts make themselves known. You might hear the phantom sounds of horses, drums, gunfire, cannons, shouting, clashing swords, screaming, and even campfire conversation. Smells drift about, including decaying flesh, sweat, blood, leather oil, cooking food, and churned up earth. Phantom forms of soldiers and animals play out scenes from the gruesome fighting. Strange mists and orbs appear and disappear without explanation.

In town many buildings are haunted as well, especially those that served as temporary hospitals and morgues.

Many of these ghosts are imprints—recordings on an endless replay loop. Some areas are particularly active on anniversary dates of the fighting. Some paranormal researchers also believe that Gettysburg is home to stuck souls: soldiers who died so violently and suddenly that they are frozen in disbelief.

Certainly the scale, and perhaps even the importance, of Gettysburg may explain why it is so haunted. But there were accounts of ghosts in the area even before the Civil War. Even during the fighting, soldiers in the Union Army's Fifth Corps saw a ghostly vision of the dead George Washington! The general who won the American Revolutionary War and became the first president of the new nation was seen in his uniform riding his horse at the head of the Fifth Corps' column as they marched. The men took the ghost as a sign from heaven that Washington had returned to help lead the Union to victory.[1]

Mark Nesbitt, a historian, author, and the leading expert on the ghosts of Gettysburg, thinks that the battlefield and surrounding area may be exceptionally haunted for other reasons. One reason may be electrical energy naturally created in the brain. At the time of death, especially a death resulting from violence, the brain might send off a tremendous burst of electricity that literally sticks in psychic space or even the land itself. That brings us to another possible reason: the content of soil. The Gettysburg soil has a high content of quartz, a mineral often associated with hauntings. Many paranormal investigators believe that quartz may act like a battery that holds the psychic energy of hauntings. Scientific research of geomagnetic fields generated by quartz and magnetic rock and soil has shown links between places of high levels of geomagnetic energy and paranormal phenomena. For more information, see the sidebar, "Are Ghosts Just in Your Head?" in Chapter 3.[2]

More recent wars and battles also have left ghostly scars. World War I and World War II ghosts remain —and not just on battlefields. For example, in England, the sounds of World War II bomber planes can still be heard at airfields where the planes once took off and landed. One-seventh of all of Britain's war casualties happened in bombing raids. In all, 300,000 raids were flown out of the country.

At Biggin Hill airfield in Kent, England, phantom figures dressed in World War II uniforms are seen and sounds of Spitfire planes are heard. There is even the ghostly sound of an airplane in distress roaring down, followed by a terrible crash, and then silence. Biggin Hill was a favorite target of German bombers.

As armed conflicts continue, battle ghosts will continue to be created. They are sad reminders of the violence and intensity of war.

Animal Ghosts and Phantimals

$\mathcal{J}$t is said that midnight marks the witching hour, the time when ghosts and creatures of the night rule the land of the living. In certain places haunted by the dead, phantoms roam from midnight until the first rays of dawn.

If you find yourself along the Hudson River at Storm King Pass in upstate New York, try to make your courage last until at least the witching hour. You just might catch a glimpse of Nab, a mighty, magnificent spectral horse, flying across the shadowy hills. Riding him is another ghost: Major General Mad Anthony Wayne, a hero of the American Revolutionary War (1775-1783). Wayne was known far and wide as "Mad Anthony" because he took outrageous risks and exhibited great daring and courage. Nab was his fearless partner. At Storm King Pass in 1779, Wayne and Nab raced along the Hudson River to warn American troops of approaching British soldiers. They still replay the scene, charging through the nightscape, showing no fear. Blue and orange sparks flash from the hooves of the phantom steed, and Wayne's dark cloak billows behind him. But if you see them, they won't see you. Wayne and Nab are imprints. They perform the same drama over and over, caught in a timeless loop.

Animal ghosts like Nab are as common as human ghosts. They haunt houses, buildings, and landscapes. This chapter looks at

Black Dogs and Demon Dogs

Late on a Saturday night Beth and Jeremy are heading home to Hagerstown, Maryland. Jeremy is driving his dad's SUV. A fog has settled over the road that runs through the hilly South Mountain terrain. The area is famous as a haunted place, and the fog intensifies the spookiness of the night. Ghosts are very much on the minds of the teens; they've just been on a ghost tour of Harpers Ferry, West Virginia, a town known for its Civil War–era ghosts.

There aren't many other cars on the road, and Jeremy's headlight beams don't penetrate the fog very far ahead. All of a sudden a dark shape looms out of the mist. It's a huge dog with enormous paws, smack in the middle of the road. Its glowing yellow eyes stare straight at Jeremy.

Beth screams as she sees the dog, too. Jeremy slams on the brakes and swerves, knowing that he's probably going to hit the creature, which is too close. The SUV shudders with the sickening thump of impact. Jeremy stops, and the shaken teens get out and look behind them, half expecting to find the mangled body of a dog. They are shocked to find no trace of the animal, alive or dead. There is no damage, not even a scratch, to the SUV.

Jeremy and Beth have just had a frightful encounter with the Snarly Yow—South Mountain's famous spectral black dog.

Phantom black dogs are well known in ghost lore all over the world. They lope about lonely country roads, along seashores, in graveyards, and in remote forested areas and fields. In some areas it's bad luck to see one; they are omens of misfortune and even death.

Black dogs are huge—bigger than even the largest breeds. They have fiery yellow, green, or red eyes, and sometimes their entire body glows with an eerie light. They go by many names, such as devil dogs, demon dogs, hellhounds, and yell hounds. In Devon, England, the Whisht hounds are headless black dogs that roam the moors with their master, the pagan god Odin. ("Whisht" means "spooky.")

Figure 6.1 *Spectral black dogs, like this artist's interpretation, are said to roam remote areas all over the world. In some regions they are considered to be signs of misfortune and death.* (Fortean Picture Library)

The most famous black dog in English lore is the fearsome Black Shuck, a calf-sized dog whose eyes are red even though t has no head. A phantom collar of chains rattles as it runs. Black Shuck is also called Galleytrot, the Hateful Thing, the Shug Monkey, Hellbeast, and the Churchyard Beast.

Many people have experiences like Jeremy and Beth. They drive along lonely roads at night, and a black dog lunges out in front of them or suddenly appears in the middle of the road. Sometimes there is a sensation of impact, and sometimes vehicles just drive right through the apparition. In earlier times before the automobile, phantom black dogs frightened the horses of nighttime travelers.

(continues)

(continued)

The origins of many black dogs are lost in time. They may have been once regarded as guardians of places. Their black color and terrible appearance have demonic associations and make them natural companions for the Devil, demons, sorcerers, and witches. In England and other parts of Europe, phantom black dogs once were blamed for livestock killings.

Sir Arthur Conan Doyle, the creator of Sherlock Holmes, drew on the legends of Black Shuck and the Whisht hounds in his tale *The Hounds of the Baskervilles.*

different types of animal ghosts and at another kind of spectral animal that seems to be a cross between phantoms and living animals: the phantimals.

ANIMAL GHOSTS

Most animal ghosts are like the ghosts of people: they are imprints or remnants of a creature that once was alive in the physical world. Animal ghosts often haunt places where they lived. They do not seem to have awareness or intelligence, but replay activities and scenes from their previous lives, like Nab. They may be seen alone or, more often, with the ghosts of people associated with them during life. For example, a ghost farmer rides down a road in a cart pulled by his ghost horse. Or the ghosts of a boy and his dog are seen playing in a house or yard where they lived.

Any animal can become a ghost, but certain animals are seen more often in phantom form. Horse ghosts are common, perhaps because people have had close relationships with horses for many centuries. People have depended upon horses for transportation, work, and pleasure. Phantom horse-drawn coaches and carriages are frequent in ghost lore. Nab has plenty of company with other ghostly galloping horses that are closely tied to their owners. In English ghost lore, the dangerous highwayman William Nevison, who lived in the seventeenth century, forever rides his spectral horse, Black Bess, between York and London. Dick Turpin, another infamous highwayman who lived in the eighteenth century, is often seen in the dark countryside around Hounslow Heath, galloping on his spectral black horse as he looks for unwary travelers to rob. The ghost of American Revolutionary War hero Paul Revere still rides his ghost horse through the New England countryside to alert people to the arrival of British troops.

Horse ghosts also are found at old battlefields. Before the age of tanks and vehicles, soldiers fought on foot and on horseback. Thousands of horses were killed in major battles. Their ghosts can be seen and heard in imprint hauntings that replay the battles.

Dogs and cats are common animal ghosts, too. Both have enjoyed close relationships with people for thousands of years. People's emotional connection to them may help imprints to linger on long after the animals themselves have lived and died.

Other kinds of animal ghost imprints are associated with activities that took place at haunted locations. For example, Charleton House is a stately home in Greenwich, near London, England. It was built in the seventeenth century as a luxurious private residence. During World War I (1914 to 1918), it was turned into a hospital. Today it is a huge office building. Charleton House is haunted by many ghosts that have interested paranormal researchers. Among the phantom residents are the ghosts of rabbits that have been seen hopping around certain parts of the building. It may seem odd that a fancy house should have rabbit ghosts in it, but many years ago, rabbits were in fact raised in one of the large rooms. Apparently, some of them decided to stay on!

Figure 6.2 *A ghostly dog can be seen in the lower left corner of this alleged spirit photograph.* (Fortean Picture Library)

The ghosts are imprints, however. They do not seem to be aware of living people, only their ghostly world.

Some animal ghosts do seem to interact with the living. This is especially the case with pets. Many people who have lost a beloved pet say they are visited by the ghost of that pet. The return visit is taken as a sign of a loving emotional bond that continues after death. People may hear, smell, or see their pet, and even feel a physical but invisible presence. Such visits are usually very comforting and can help ease a person's grief.

Joshua P. Warren is a paranormal researcher who lives in North Carolina. When his miniature dachshund, Nellie, died, she came back as a ghost. Warren heard her familiar whimpers and barks in empty rooms in his house and also heard the sounds of her little toenails on the hardwood floor. He did not see Nellie but felt a strong sense of her presence on several occasions. Nellie's ghost remained for about a week and then faded away. Warren tried to capture evidence of Nellie with photographic and recording equipment but was not successful. However, he was firmly convinced from his own experiences that Nellie had in fact returned in a ghostly way to visit him.[1]

Experiences such as Warren's have been reported by so many people that it is difficult to explain them away as imagination or wishful thinking as a result of sorrow and grief. If it is possible for people to return after death as ghosts for purposeful visits, then perhaps it is possible for animals to do the same.

Descriptions of visits by pet ghosts fall into certain patterns. The ghosts usually make themselves known soon after death and for a short period of time, such as a few days or a week or two. The ghosts behave as the animals did when they were alive. For example, a ghost cat may be glimpsed as it jumps up on a sofa or bed. A bird may be heard chirping in the room where it was caged. Often, the ghost animals are not seen but are heard, smelled, and sensed.

As time passes the strength of their ghostly presence weakens until it stops altogether. Sometimes people report that their dead pets return for visits for years. A small number of pet owners say they feel a constant presence of their departed pets.

Not all pets return to their owners as ghosts. The reasons why some do and some do not are not known. Wishing for the ghost of a pet will not necessarily make it appear.

PHANTIMALS

Some phantom animals are not the ghosts of the dead but belong to a special supernatural realm. Phantimals—a word coined by Joshua P. Warren—look and act ghostly, but their appearances and characteristics may be due to the fact that they do not belong to the physical realm. According to folklore traditions that go back to ancient times, there are realms populated by magical or supernatural creatures that have the ability to pop in and out of our world.

One type of phantimal is the elemental animal. These are phantom-like creatures that are similar to, but not quite the same as, ordinary animals. An example is the phantom black dogs and demon dogs reported in many locations around the world (see sidebar). These creatures look like dogs but are huge in size, with supernatural characteristics, such as fiery red eyes and the ability to disappear in a moment. The same applies to other elemental animal phantoms: they resemble ordinary animals but often have scary features and characteristics. They appear and disappear in and out of the ordinary world. They are usually seen out in the wild, especially in remote and lonely areas.

Some paranormal experts think that elemental animals are real creatures that exist in their own real world, like another dimension that is very close to ours. These creatures occasionally come through doorways between the dimensions. Animal spirits worshiped as deities in some cultures may be related to elemental animals.

Another type of phantimal is the familiar, a spectral animal that serves as a reliable spirit helper or magical helper to people. Some familiars are said to be the spirits of dead animals who return to serve their owners or masters. Other familiars are summoned from the spirit worlds through magic. Because they exist in a phantom realm, familiars are capable of traveling great distances quickly, and they can do things that living people and animals cannot do. In magic, they deliver messages and help carry out spells. They can shape-shift to different forms, such as various kinds of animals and even insects.

Familiars are part of ancient magical and shamanic traditions. They are not evil in nature, but they can be directed to do things that are either good or bad. In Europe during the late Middle Ages, many people were afraid of witches. They believed that witches commanded demons who took the forms of animals and became their familiars.

A third type of phantimal is the cryptid. The term cryptid comes from cryptozoology, the study of mysterious or "hidden" creatures.

Bigfoot or Sasquatch is a cryptid, and so is the Loch Ness Monster. Cryptids seem to be real but strange creatures, but no one ever seems to find concrete proof of their existence. Like elemental animals they act like ghosts because they probably do not live entirely in the physical world. They appear and disappear suddenly. They have supernatural powers and abilities.

Some cryptids seem to be weird hybrids. For example, people have reported seeing creatures that appear to be half human and half animal. Such creatures have existed in mythology since ancient times. In Greek mythology one of the best-known hybrids is the centaur, which has the lower body of a horse and the upper body of a man. Dog men, who have human bodies with dog or wolf heads and other features, also are found in many folklore traditions, including in North America. Half human and half bird creatures have been reported as well.

In 1966 a creature known as Mothman was sighted in West Virginia and along the Ohio River. It had the body of a man and large wings like a bat or bird. But it did not fly like an ordinary bat or bird. Mothman rose straight up in the air without flapping its wings. Mothman terrified people for a short period of time. The creature never threatened or attacked people, but its appearance was scary enough.

Other weird things happened during the same period. There were numerous reports of UFO sightings and extraterrestrial, or E.T., contacts. People had disruptions in their telephones service and problems with electrical equipment. A reporter named John Keel received prophecies of disasters from sources who identified themselves as E.T.s. The phenomena came to a crashing halt on December 15, 1967, when a bridge across the Ohio River collapsed, killing 46 people. Was the collapse connected to the phenomena? No one knows for certain, and opinions are still divided.

The Mothman hauntings serve as an example of how paranormal phenomena sometimes occur in clusters or blend together. Ghosts are not always alone.

7

Nasty Hauntings

The newspapers called it the "House of Demons." J. P. Manrow called it unbearable. When Manrow built his home on Russian Hill in San Francisco in 1851, he had no idea that it would house more than his family. Unfriendly spirits moved right in with him. Manrow, a civil engineer who made a fortune in California real estate, expected to live the high life. Instead, he found himself at the mercy of invisible pranksters.

Troubling things happened from the family's first day in the house. Something kept stealing objects and hiding them or moving them around. Mrs. Manrow seemed to be the favorite target. She would come home from shopping, set her purchases down, turn away for a moment—and they would be gone. Later, she would find them in a strange place in the house.

Once the family was rudely surprised by salt in the sugar bowl instead of sugar. Imagine putting sugar on your cereal and finding that you'd loaded it with salt instead! And there were unexplained rapping sounds coming from within the walls. The sounds disturbed and frightened the family at all hours of the day and night.

The family soon tired of the tricks and weird noises, but the intrusions would not stop. They went on for years.

By 1856 Manrow was at his wit's end. He told a few friends about his ghostly problems. The men thought it would be a good idea to investigate. They decided to hold an amateur séance at Manrow's home with their wives present. No one knew how to organize or control a séance, and the group got far more than they bargained for. The table levitated. Objects were tossed about the room. Everyone was pinched and had their hair pulled. The doorbell rang by itself.

Most frightening of all was the appearance of a demonic-looking apparition outside the house. The horrible figure stared at them through a window. A local newspaper dubbed Manrow's home the "House of Demons," giving a colorful description of it:

> If all the fiends in hell had combined their features into one master-piece of ugliness and revolting hideousness of countenance, they could not have produced a face so full of horrors. It was blacker than the blackest midnight that ever frowned in starless gloom over the storm-swept ocean.[1]

If this wasn't terrifying enough, the group decided to hold two more séances. Once they attempted to ask "good" spirits to come and push out the bad spirits. All they did was stir up more violent poltergeist activity.

After three séances they gave up. The Manrow family just put up with all the ghostly activity for the rest of their time in the house.

The Manrow House no longer exists, having been replaced by an apartment tower. No explanation for the haunting was ever found, so the question remains: why would a brand new house be occupied by any ghosts or spirits, let alone unfriendly ones? Strangely, this sort of negative haunting happens over and over again, in both old and brand new houses today. Sometimes the ghosts or spirits seem attached to the place, and sometimes they seem attached to specific people.

Take, for example, the tragic Jaboticabal poltergeist case.

"Poltergeist" is a German term for "noisy spirit." It is used to describe hauntings in which things are thrown and people are attacked by invisible biting, scratching, and pinching. There may be interference with equipment. Sometimes poltergeists are identified as

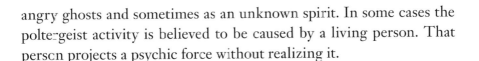

angry ghosts and sometimes as an unknown spirit. In some cases the poltergeist activity is believed to be caused by a living person. That person projects a psychic force without realizing it.

A TRAGIC END TO A POLTERGEIST ATTACK

The Jaboticabal case took place in the 1960s in Jaboticabal, Brazil. The cause of the disturbances identified itself as an angry spirit who was taking revenge on the victim, an 11-year-old girl.

The haunting started in 1965 when bricks fell into the home of Maria Jose Ferreira. The bricks seemed to come from nowhere. After several days of falling bricks, the family believed an evil spirit was present. They called a priest to do an exorcism, but it only made things worse. Bricks and stones continued to crash through the house, followed by eggs, dishes, other household objects, and even furniture.

Poor Maria was the center of the attacks. She was slapped, bruised, and bitten by unseen attackers. Once she was attacked with needles that suddenly appeared embedded in her skin. One day while she was eating her lunch at school, her clothing began to smolder.

After a year of unrelenting attacks, Maria was taken to a medium. The medium said she was the victim of an angry ghost who claimed that in a previous life, Maria had been a witch who had killed the person. The ghost pledged to make Maria suffer.

No remedies stopped the attacks. Five years after the problems started, Maria was found dead of poisoning; she is believed to have ended her own misery. All the poltergeist activity stopped after Maria's death.

AMITYVILLE: ONE OF THE WORST HAUNTINGS ON RECORD

Finally, let's take a look at one of the most famous nasty hauntings of all time: the Amityville case. A great deal of controversy has raged over how much of this case actually happened. Lawsuits were filed

The Curse of the Bell Witch

Betsy Bell was just another farm girl in rural America—until a witch's curse turned her life into a living nightmare. The year was 1817, and Betsy was 12 years old.

The supernatural attacks began suddenly, starting with the appearances of weird creatures, a dog-like thing and a turkey-like bird, on the Bell farm in Adams, Tennessee. The dog creature disappeared when Betsy's father, John, fired a gun at it.

Bizarre things started happening at the Bell farmhouse. Loud raps and knocks sounded on the doors and windows though no one was there. Sounds like giant rats chewing on the bedposts were heard, as well as sounds like the claws of giant dogs digging on the floors.

The disturbances went on for a year, affecting Betsy, her seven brothers and sisters, and parents John and Lucy. Then things took a severe turn for the worse, and Betsy was the main target. At night invisible hands ripped away her bed covers. The unseen hands slapped her, pinched her, and stuck her with pins. She had bruises all over her body. Every night the poor girl suffered from an attacker she could not see.

A spirit voice soon identified itself as the source of the trouble. First the spirit claimed to be millions of years old and "from everywhere." Then it said it was the ghost of an immigrant who was going to show Betsy where to find money. Then it said it was "old Kate Batts's witch," and its purpose was to torment John Bell for the rest of his life, and to prevent Betsy from marrying a young man named Josh Gardner. Kate Batts was a real woman, a neighbor who supposedly did not get along with John Bell. Many people believed Old Kate cursed the Bells. Historial documents, however, indicate that Kate Batts had little contact with John Bell and that she outlived him by many years, which would make it impossible for her ghost to have been behind the haunting.

The torments went on for three years. No one was able to help the Bells. John's health declined, and he finally died on December 19, 1820. His family believed he was somehow poisoned by the invisible spirit.

Figure 7.1   *The Bell Witch Cave. Some say it is an interdimensional portal responsible for the Bell Witch phenomena.* (Author's collection)

Betsy announced her engagement to Josh, which brought on a fresh round of attacks. At last she gave in, and broke the engagement. She married another man.

The Bell Witch plagued many other people in the community, but Betsy got the worst of the attacks. Some modern experts think she was a living poltergeist agent, unwittingly full of repressed energy due to her strict Baptist upbringing. Others say the spirit was riled up over the desecration of Native American burial grounds nearby. Still others think that "something" came through an interdimensional portal in a nearby cave.

The cause of the Bell Witch may never be known. But the former Bell farm remains haunted to this day, including the cave where "Old Kate Batt's witch" was said to hide. Visitors report noises, voices, taps, raps, and mysterious photographic effects.

over it. But *something* drove the Lutz family out of their new home in Amityville, Long Island, New York.

George and Kathy Lutz were newlyweds when they found the house in December 1975. They didn't have much money, and the house was a bargain. It was cheap because of horrific murders that had been committed there 13 months earlier. Ronald DeFeo, 23, was convicted of second-degree murder for the gun slayings of six members of his family: his parents, two brothers, and two sisters. At the time the Lutz family bought the house, DeFeo was in prison.

The Lutzes had barely moved in when dark and sinister things started happening. Disembodied voices ordered them to get out. Kathy's three children from her previous marriage were terrified. Swarms of flies came into the house. Kathy had nightmares about the murders. The family saw a ghostly demon boy who could shape-shift into a demonic pig. Green slime oozed from walls. Strange noises were heard in the middle of the night.

Many more awful things happened, according to the Lutzes. They tried to bless the house with prayer, but it had no effect. After 28 days they had a terror-filled night and could stand no more. They packed a few belongings and got out.

The case was investigated by the famous husband-and-wife demonologist team, Ed and Lorraine Warren, and some prominent paranormal investigators, including Hans Holzer. Media publicity made the Lutzes and the house famous.

In the aftermath the Lutzes were accused of making up their story in order to sell a book or movie idea. They did sell their story, but they stood their ground that their claims were true. Author Jay Anson wrote a best-selling book about the case, *The Amityville Horror* (1977). Unfortunately there were errors in the book. Skeptics used the errors as an argument that the case was a hoax.

Numerous lawsuits were filed by different parties over claims and accusations. Legal issues went on for years. Meanwhile the house was under siege by a steady stream of curiosity-seekers.

Figure 7.2 *The home of the murdered Defeo family in Amityville, NY, was said to be haunted after their deaths.* (Bettmann/Corbis)

Despite the controversy and criticisms, the Lutzes stuck to their story. But the turmoil took its toll, and they divorced in the 1980s. Kathy died in 2004, and George died in 2006.

Anson's book was made into a hit film. Several other "Amityville" books and films have come out, and the name "Amityville Horror" has even been made a legal trademark.

Was the haunting real? Were the murders the cause or did something invade the house for another reason? No one has the answer. The phenomena described by the Lutzes have been documented in other negative hauntings. The Lutzes were criticized and pressured by skeptics for years, yet they did not back down. Whatever happened, it was enough to force them out and to endure years of public controversy.

Nasty hauntings do happen, but fortunately they are not common. They are not imprints, like most hauntings. Explanations that have

Getting Rid of Ghosts

*E*veryone loves a good ghost story, but few people want to live with a ghost, even an imprint. Cold spots, unexplained sounds, shadows, movements of objects, and other phenomena can be annoying or frightening.

Since ancient times people have had ways of getting rid of ghosts. Different terms have been used for these remedies, such as "ghost laying," **"ghost releasement,"** and even "exorcism." Sometimes people consult experts to do the job. Sometimes they practice "do-it-yourself" ghost laying. If you have a pesky ghost, what should you do?

First, make certain as best as you can that there is no natural explanation. Many odd sounds, smells, cold spots, and so on do have natural causes. They are not automatically signs of ghosts.

You also must honestly ask yourself if your own imagination is involved. It's easy to fill in blanks. Sometimes it's tempting to have a ghost story and be a center of attention.

f a haunting involves attacks, such as the throwing of objects, pinches, bruises, and even bad dreams, it's wise to consult an expert.

The following remedies are useful:

1   *Ask the ghost to leave.* It may seem too simple, but it works. Be polite but firm. The physical world belongs to the living, and so you have the upper hand. As an alternative you can ask the ghost not to bother you. Make it clear you don't mind if it shares your space, but you do not wish to be disturbed.

2   *Cleanse and purify.* Take a lighted white candle and go from room to room. Tell all unwanted presences to leave immediately. Seal each room by visualizing white light around it. Make a prayer for

protection. Some ghost experts burn sage and other herbs to
cleanse rooms.

3   *Redecorate.* Changing a space can disrupt haunting patterns. Rear-
range furniture. New paint, carpeting, cabinetry, and room remodel-
ing are especially good for disrupting hauntings.

4   *Use crystals.* In folklore dark, heavy stones repel ghosts. Place pieces
of obsidian, hematite, black onyx, and jet around the home.

5   *Do feng shui.* The Chinese "art of placement" concerns changing the
physical environment to minimize negative energies and maximize
positive ones. Shapes, colors, textures, mirrors, fountains, and crystals are common tools to change the energy of place. For removing
ghosts, it's best to consult a feng shui expert.

6   *Get experienced help.* Consult an expert on ghost releasement. Many
ghost hunters and paranormal research organizations have, or know
of, such experts. Do not attempt to do a séance on your own. Results can be unpredictable. Only experienced and qualified persons
should conduct séances.

7   *Get out the beans.* That's right. Beans have long been associated
with the dead. The Romans offered beans to the dead to propitiate
them and exorcise them. In Japanese lore roasted beans are scattered about the house in a New Year's ritual to drive out ghosts
and demons and bring in luck. In the folklore of many places,
beans—or small seeds such as poppy or millet—are scattered across
a door threshold to keep ghosts away. According to lore the ghosts
must stop and pick up or count every bean or seed, which keeps
them busy. This tactic is employed against vampires, too. A multi-
purpose remedy!

been put forward for them include angry ghosts, poltergeists, and demons and other spirits. Sometimes the reasons for the hauntings seem obvious, and solutions are found. Other times, nasty hauntings eventually end on their own. Occasionally they continue regardless of the efforts of people to end them. They are one of the mysteries within a mystery, reinforcing how little is known and understood about the paranormal.

Ghosts on Camera

Williillam Mumler was a Boston jeweler's engraver and amateur photographer of no particular skill, until one fateful day when a strange photograph changed his life and made him famous.

Toiling away alone in a studio on October 5, 1861, the 29-year-old Mumler had no idea of the fantastic image that was about to develop on his plate. He had just finished taking portraits of himself. The process was long and difficult. First he had to prepare his plates by coating them with collodion (a chemical solution), then bathing them in silver nitrate, and then taking the photographs while the plates were still wet. He had to sit very still during the actual photographing.

When he examined his results, Mumler was shocked to see that in one photograph, a pale image of a young woman appeared next to him on his right. At first he thought he had used a previously exposed plate that had not been cleaned properly. Mumler showed the photograph around. It caused a sensation. Spiritualism, which focused on communication with the spirit world and proving that there is an afterlife, was at a peak of popularity. A photograph of the dead surely was ironclad proof that spirits survived after death. For many Spiritualists, Mumler became an instant celebrity.

Mumler was not the first person to take a spirit photograph. In 1860 W. Campbell, of Jersey City, New Jersey, exhibited a photograph he took of an empty chair. When developed it showed the ghost of a boy. But Campbell was never able to take another spirit photograph, even though he tried. Fame is often a matter of being in the right place at the right time. This was the case for Mumler, and he got the buzz. Spirit photography was born.

Caught up in the excitement, Mumler said that he recalled that during the sitting, he had experienced an electrical trembling in his right arm that had left him exhausted. He recognized the young woman in the photo as a cousin who had died 12 years earlier. He could not explain how a dead person, not visible when the photograph was taken, had managed to show up in the developed image. It was a great mystery!

Mumler was besieged by people who wanted their photographs taken in the hopes that their dearly departed would show up, too. Overnight he went from an unknown amateur photographer to a celebrity earning top dollar. Not everyone jumped on the bandwagon, however. Some suspected trickery.

One skeptic was William Black, an esteemed Boston photographer. He sat for a photograph with Mumler and kept a careful eye on the procedure. He wanted to make sure that Mumler didn't switch plates. To Black's astonishment his photograph showed an "extra"—a ghostly young man leaning over his shoulder. The skeptic was converted. Mumler, Black proclaimed, had a gift for making spirits appear on film.

Giddy with his instant fame, Mumler moved to New York City, advertised himself as a medium, and began charging the outrageous sum of $10 per sitting, with no guarantees. He had no shortage of customers. Even his wife, Hannah, got into the act. Suddenly, she, too, was a medium who could see the spirits before they were photographed. She described her visions to customers in advance of their sittings.

One of Mumler's most famous clients was Mary Todd Lincoln, the grief-stricken widow of President Abraham Lincoln. Mrs. Lincoln visited Mumler under the assumed name of Mrs. Lindall in hopes that her assassinated husband would show up in a photograph.

She was not disappointed. In the photo Mumler took of Mrs. Lincoln, the dead president appeared standing behind her, his ghostly hands resting upon her shoulders as she gazed solemnly into the camera.

In spite of his fans Mumler continued to be hounded by skeptics who believed he was committing a clever fraud. He became so controversial that he was finally arrested and charged with fraud in 1869. At a preliminary trial his case was dismissed. Did he ever resort to tricks? No one knows. But as often happens with instant fame, the fall is just as swift as the rocket ride up. Mumler's personal life fell apart. He and Hannah divorced, and he ended his days in poverty and obscurity, dying in 1884.

PHOTOGRAPH OF MRS. LINCOLN, with spirit of Abraham Lincoln and Son. BY MUMLER, BOSTON, U.S.A. Copied by Hudson. See "Human Nature," December, 1874.

Figure 8.1 *William Mumler's photograph of the spirit of Abraham Lincoln with his hands on his wife's shoulders.* (Mary Evans Picture Library)

Mumler's ability to produce results set in motion an entire industry of spirit photography. Other photographers, eager to make fast money, promised spirit photographs to a believing public. Some were indeed outright frauds, doctoring plates with phony images of famous dead people and supposed Native American spirit guides wearing enormous feather headdresses. Ghostly faces were shown floating in neat semicircles over the heads of living subjects. Pale forms trailed filmy white garments.

The craze traveled across the Atlantic Ocean and took hold in Great Britain and Europe as well. Spirit photography was all the rage for decades. Some mediums said they could cause spirit images to be impressed on *unexposed* plates. These images were called "scotographs" and sometimes contained messages allegedly written by the hands of the spirits themselves.

In 1905 a new star rose: William Hope, a carpenter who lived in Crewe, England. Hope took his first spirit photograph that year and went on to take more than 2,500 photographs over the next 20 years. Hope was accused of fraud, and evidence did point in that direction. Among his accusers was Harry Price, who was yet to become famous for his investigation of haunted Borley Rectory (see Chapter 10). Price said he observed Hope switching plates during his session.

In fact, creating fraudulent spirit photographs was all too easy. Various tricks of doctored plates and double exposures had been in use since the 1850s to make unusual photographs for "entertainment purposes." Ghosts, floating furniture, and other supposedly paranormal effects such as phantom mists looked real, but were not.

Even children could fake spirit photographs. Between 1917 and 1920 Sir Arthur Conan Doyle was fooled by two school girls in Cottingley, Yorkshire, England, in what became known as the Cottingley Fairies scandal. The girls, Francis Griffiths and Elsie Wright, said they could photograph the many fairies they played with. The girls created the fairies from cutouts from a book. Doyle was a towering figure in Spiritualism and was renowned for his fiction, as the creator of the famous sleuth Sherlock Holmes. Somehow he was taken in by the fraud. When he publicly proclaimed the photos genuine, he became a laughingstock on both sides of the Atlantic. It was a humiliating experience. The girls stuck to their story, but in the 1980s they finally admitted to hoaxing the photos. They said they did it to get back at adults who ridiculed them for seeing fairies.

Eventually fraud and improved technology put an end to the early days of spirit photography. Photography and the paranormal moved to the séance room.

Figure 8.2 *William Hope's photograph of Harry Price with an alleged spirit. Price challenged the authenticity of this picture.* (Mary Evans Picture Library)

Orbs: Fake Ghosts or the Real Deal?

Just what *are* those fuzzy round globes of light that show up in photographs, especially ones taken at night? Many people believe they are ghosts or spirits or at least something associated with them.

But paranormal investigators are very skeptical of orbs, believing that nearly all of them have natural explanations. The natural causes are merely misinterpreted by people who are eager to see evidence of ghosts and spirits.

Orbs are controversial, with believers and skeptics firmly entrenched in their views. The evidence, however, tilts toward the skeptics. Orbs were practically unknown before the digital camera became popular. True, mysterious lights and luminosities have been captured since the invention of photography. But digital cameras and ever-tinier film cameras have brought an explosion of orb photos. Therein lie the problems, say the experts. Orbs have more to do with technology and nature than the paranormal.

Here are the most common causes of orbs.

- pixilation flaws in digital cameras. The orb is a spot of missing pixels, which get filled in as fuzzy blobs. Older cameras are more prone to this problem than newer cameras, which have higher pixel resolutions.
- light reflections and refractions
- particles so close to the camera lens that they are out of focus, such as dust, pollen, water droplets, humidity, and insects

MEDIUMS, MATERIALIZATIONS AND LEVITATIONS

The age of Spiritualism, which started in the late 1840s, ushered in an age of physical mediumship. By the late nineteenth century

- foreign material on or within the camera lens, such as tiny pieces of lint or dirt

- real lights that seem mysterious when photographed

Sometimes even large objects, such as strands of hair hanging in front of the lens, fingers in front of the lens, and loose camera lens covers on strings can look like "moving orbs." However, they are merely out of focus, which can create trails. Orbs that are rectangular or octagonal in shape have taken on the shape of the lens of the camera. The person taking the photo may not be aware of such factors at the time, but interpret them as paranormal when they see the photo.

Orbs that show up in daytime shots are most likely lens flares and slow shutter speeds.

The construction of newer cameras may be one reason why orbs show up more often than in the past. Compact cameras have flash units much closer to the lens and have the power to throw up to three times longer flash beams than older and bigger cameras. The edge of the flash beam passes much closer to the lens and decreases the angle of reflection back into the lens. Thus, the camera has a higher likelihood of producing flares and orbs.

Nonetheless, even the skeptics say that not all orbs have natural explanations. Some may be an unknown psychic or spiritual energy, or energy of place, or they may be a by-product of hauntings. Some orbs are associated with extraterrestrial activity, too.

psychical research became an organized field. Leading scientists and philosophers joined groups such as the Society for Psychical Research in London and the American Society for Psychical Research in New York City to investigate mediums and the paranormal and look for proof of survival.

In séances mediums attempted to open communication with the dead, who would prove their reality by producing paranormal phenomena. For example, the spirits allegedly would make unusual noises or cause objects to levitate or move. The best mediums claimed to produce materialized spirits, such as ghostly hands and forms that appeared in the séance room. Some materialized spirits moved about the rooms and even touched the sitters present. Another highly rated phenomenon was ectoplasm, a mysterious white substance that oozed from a medium's body and hung in strings or froths, and sometimes turned into materialized spirits.

Photographing the evidence produced by mediums was not easy, for most mediums worked in the dark—a condition necessary for communicating with the spirit world, they said. Investigators set up arrays of cameras in séance rooms that would flash periodically or when set off by an investigator.

Some séance photographs looked a lot like early "extras" photographs: suspicious. Some spirit forms looked like cardboard cutouts. Ectoplasm looked like cloth. And full-formed materialized spirits looked remarkably alive. Many mediums were exposed as frauds. Some of them impersonated the spirits themselves or had helpers do it. One of the most famous photographed spirits was Katie King, materialized by Agnes Guppy in the 1870s. Mrs. Guppy, as she was known, claimed to be the first medium in England to produce spirits. Katie and her ghost father, John, were controversial. Skeptics said Katie was really Guppy in disguise.

Not all photographs of séance-room phenomena could be explained, however. In Winnipeg, Manitoba, Canada, investigator Thomas Glendenning Hamilton took some astonishing photographs in the 1920s of ectoplasm and levitating tables. The photographs have never been debunked.

The golden age of physical mediumship ended around the 1930s, replaced by mental mediumship, or channeled messages. By then

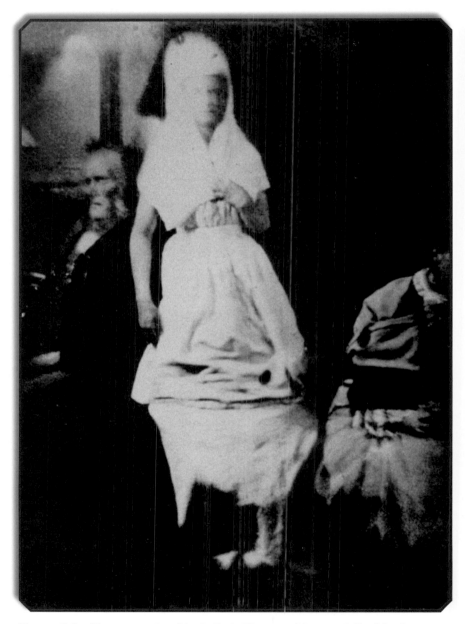

Figure 8.3 *The woman in white is Katie King, a spirit materialized by Agnes Guppy. Some say Katie was really Agnes in disguise.* (Fortean Picture Library)

psychical researchers and ghost hunters were taking their cameras into haunted places.

GHOST PHOTOS

Ghost hunters love nothing more than getting solid evidence that ghosts exist. Photographs are the best evidence. But capturing ghosts in photos is hard to do. Ghosts just don't pose on command. For decades the only procedures investigators could use was to set up surveillance video cameras, snap lots of still images, and hope for the best. Even when something unusual, such as a shadowy or filmy form, or mysterious lights, shows up in a photograph, there may be natural explanations. Proving you've photographed ghosts is difficult.

Some of the best photographs of possible paranormal phenomena have been taken unintentionally and by amateurs. People who take photographs of other people or of activities or landscapes are sometimes surprised to see that something shows up that shouldn't be in the photo. Every year paranormal investigators examine thousands of photographs sent to them by curious people wanting to know if they've photographed a ghost. Most such photos involve lights, mists, fogs, and streaking objects. But some—a tiny minority—show forms that seem to be from another realm.

The photo of the Brown Lady of Raynham Hall has never been debunked since it was taken in 1936. Raynham Hall, a manor house near Fakenham, Norfolk, England, has been haunted for more than 250 years by the Brown Lady. The ghost's identity is not certain. She is believed to be Lady Dorothy Townsend, who lived there in the early eighteenth century. Her ghost is called the Brown Lady because she appears in a brown dress.

In 1936 the Lady Townsend of the time hired a photographer to take pictures of the inside of the manor house. The photographer, Mr. Provand, was taking flash photographs of the main staircase when

Figure 8.4 *The famous Brown Lady of Raynham Hall. This photo has never been debunked.* (Fortean Picture Library)

Figure 8.5 *The Spiral Staircase Ghost of Queen's House near London.* (Mary Evans Picture Library)

his assistant, Shira, suddenly saw the Brown Lady coming down the stairs. Provand could not see the ghost himself. He pointed the camera where the excited Shira directed and snapped one of the most celebrated ghost photos in history. The photo shows a filmy form of a woman in the middle of the staircase. Many experts have examined the photo, but no evidence of fraud, or a natural explanation, has ever been determined.

In 1966 another accidental and famous ghost photo was taken at the Queen's House in Greenwich, near London. Two Canadian tourists, R. W. Hardy and his wife, were visiting the seventeenth-century house. They took numerous photographs. One photograph of the staircase shows a ghostly form leaning over the railing, even though the stairs were empty at the time. Like the photo of the Brown Lady of Raynham Hall, no explanation has been determined. Interestingly, the Queen's House has no record of being haunted!

Most modern spirit photographs are taken in digital format. Early digital photographs were easy to alter, but newer model cameras embed information in the images that makes trickery much more difficult to pull off. Still, many ghost investigators prefer to work with film cameras so that they have both hard print and negative. Or they use both digital and film. Digital has the advantage of showing the image immediately.

In 1991 an unusual ghost photograph was taken in Chicago's famous Bachelor's Grove Cemetery. The photographer, Mari Huff, was using infrared film. Her photograph, which remains unexplained, shows a semitransparent girl in an old-fashioned dress sitting on top of a broken tomb. The girl was not visible when the photograph was taken. Huff had pointed the camera into an area where paranormal activity had been reported.

Ghostly images also are captured on video and camcorder. Most are vague shapes that are either filmy white or dark shadows. They usually last only a few seconds, and they are often hard to evaluate. Sometimes natural things are mistaken for ghosts, such as background patterns and tiny objects so close to the lens that they are out of focus. Most controversial of all are orbs, mysterious balls of light (see sidebar).

The history of spirit photography has had its ups and downs. Nonetheless, photography remains one of the best tools for capturing evidence of ghosts.

Spirit Voices: Ghosts Who Are Heard but Not Seen

Ghosts are talking—but how can we hear them?

In 1959 a Swedish opera singer and film producer named Freidrich Jurgenson stumbled upon a way to hear the dead. One day he set a tape recorder outside at his country villa to record bird songs. When he played the tape back, he got more than bird songs. Captured on the tape was a clear male voice speaking in Norwegian, discussing night bird songs.

Jurgenson assumed his recorder had somehow picked up a radio broadcast. However, it was too weird that the voice was talking about bird songs, the very thing Jurgenson was trying to record. He set his recorder out again to see if the same thing happened. He sat with the recorder while it taped.

This time Jurgenson got multiple voices talking on his tape, even though he had heard no voices during the taping. To make matters stranger, the voices gave personal information about Jurgenson, and gave him instructions for how to record more voices. Jurgenson was both chilled and fascinated. Had he somehow penetrated the veil to the Other Side? Were the ghosts of the dead *right next to him*, trying to communicate, and finding a way to do so through a recorder?

For several years Jurgenson experimented with taping the disembodied voices. In 1964 he published his results in a book, *Voices from the Universe*, which came packaged with a record of some of the voices.

The effect was electrifying, launching an international field of research known as the electronic voice phenomena (EVP), the taping of unexplained voices. Today no ghost investigation is complete without trying for EVP.

EARLY EVP EFFORTS

Jurgenson was not the first to tape ghostly voices. In the early years of the twentieth century, Thomas Alva Edison, one of America's greatest inventors, believed that spirit voices could be recorded. Edison, who pioneered inventions in sound recording, telecommunications, electricity, motion pictures, mining, and other fields, was intrigued by spirit photography and felt that ghosts could be heard as well as seen. Supposedly Edison worked on inventing an EVP device, but he died in 1931 without leaving any notes or plans.

From the time of Edison to Jurgenson's discovery, other researchers attempted to record not only the voices of the dead but messages from extraterrestrials. Jurgenson's work came to the attention of a Latvian psychologist, Konstantin Raudive, who went on to record more than 100,000 voices. Raudive put EVP on the map in a big way with his best-selling book, *Breakthrough: An Amazing Experiment in Electronic Communication*, published in 1971. So influential was Raudive's work that for many years, EVP were called "Raudive voices."

On the heels of Raudive EVP came to the attention of a firm skeptic: Sarah Estep. In 1976 Estep read about the international research in *The Handbook of Psi Discoveries* by Sheila Ostrander and Lynn Schroeder. Estep did not believe in an afterlife; she was convinced that death was the final end.

Estep held this belief because of an experience she had at age five. Her grandparents owned and lived in a funeral home in Westfield, New York, and Estep and her family, who lived in Altoona, Pennsylvania, visited there every summer. The children were forbidden to go into the viewing room, where embalmed bodies were put on display in caskets so that family and friends could say their final good-byes. But one day little Estep snuck into the room and peered into a casket.

"I wasn't at all frightened," she recalled later. "They were dead and I knew they couldn't hurt me. But I became convinced that once you die, you go into a hole in the ground. Death is a casket. I grew up thinking there was no life after death. There was no heaven, no anything. I didn't dare tell my parents or anyone. I didn't like that feeling, but I couldn't think anything else because I'd seen all these dead people."[1]

With such an attitude Estep felt challenged to prove EVP voices were false. At her home in Annapolis, Maryland, she set up her own reel-to-reel tape experiments. For nearly a week she got nothing. Just as she was about to give up, she recorded a female voice that answered her with the words, "Our world is one of beauty."

Estep was hooked and went on to record about 25,000 EVP tapes, some of the dead and some, she believed, of E.T.s. In 1982 she founded the American Association-Electronic Voice Phenomena, one of the leading organizations in the world dedicated to EVP and related research. About six years into her research, Estep received a profound message when a voice told her, "Death no more a casket."

Since 2000 the AA-EVP has been directed by Tom and Lisa Butler of Reno, Nevada.

Today EVP is a popular field pursued by both amateurs and professionals around the world. Many researchers are interested in looking for evidence to prove survival after death. The communicators do not have to be tied to a particular place, but respond from wherever they are in another dimension.

In ghost hunting EVP provides evidence of presences haunting a site. Investigators ask questions related to the place and space questions so that ghosts—if they can or will communicate—can answer before another question is asked. Sometimes other phantom sounds show up, such as animal sounds, battle noises, music, and singing. It

Figure 9.1 *Sarah Estep, founder of the American Association-Electronic Voice Phenomena.* (Author's collection)

is exciting to visit a haunted place and record sounds and voices from another time or dimension.

CHARACTERISTICS OF EVP

No one knows exactly how phantom voices manage to become impressed on a tape or digital recording. Are the voices picked up by the microphone or impressed directly on tape or chip? Why are the voices seldom audible during recording? If the communicators can be recorded, why don't they just speak directly to the living? No one has any certain answers. Forensics research at Il Laboratorio in Italy shows that sounds made by EVP voices are sometimes impossible to reproduce with human vocal chords.

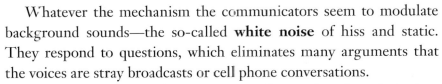

Whatever the mechanism the communicators seem to modulate background sounds—the so-called **white noise** of hiss and static. They respond to questions, which eliminates many arguments that the voices are stray broadcasts or cell phone conversations.

Estep created a classification system of voices based on their clarity. Class A voices are clearly heard and understood by most people. Class B voices are clear, but listeners may disagree over what is said. Class C voices are so faint they usually require headphones and amplification and are much harder to decipher. The majority of EVP are Class C.

Some investigators think that at least some EVP are imprints from previous times—recordings that do not change and can be listened to when the conditions are right.

INSTRUMENTAL TRANSCOMMUNICATION

A new field of research called instrumental transcommunication, or ITC, evolved from EVP. ITC includes unexplained contact involving all kinds of high technology in addition to recorders: television sets, computers, telephones, fax machines, and so forth. Voices, photos, images, computer files, and faxes are transdimensional communications, or transcommunications, that is, sent from the higher realms to the physical world of the living. Researchers say the senders are both the dead and beings who are more highly evolved than humans—what some might call angels. In ITC they are referred to as ethereal beings.

Instrumental transcommunication got its start by researchers in Europe in the 1970s and 1980s. Today there are many groups and organizations around the world pursuing research in this area. Some researchers say they can use computers to have on-demand, real-time conversations with the dead.

There are a variety of inventions that create a matrix of white noise intended for spirits to use to create their own voices for live

Do-It-Yourself EVP

Anyone can experiment with EVP. All you need is a tape recorder or a digital recorder. You don't even have to go to a haunted place. You can do it right in your own home.

You are likely to get better results if you record on a schedule. Pick a quiet time of day or night—spirit voices have no preference—that you can set aside on a regular basis. It can be every day or once a week. Record in the same place.

EVP experts agree that your mindset can also influence your results. You will do better if you take EVP seriously and want to learn something from it, rather than if you treat it like entertainment or a game. If you are tired or not feeling well, skip a session. EVP responds more to high energy.

Start your recording and announce your name, date, and time. This establishes a record. Then ask simple questions that need only short answers. Be silent after every question, which allows for answers to appear on your recorder. Some examples of questions are

• Is anyone here who would like to communicate?

communication. Such devices are controversial and have been used in experiments with both positive and negative results.

In both EVP and ITC researchers say that the consciousness, or intention, of the researchers determines the results they get. A researcher who is seriously interested in advancing knowledge will get better results than skeptics and people who just want to be entertained.

There is actually scientific evidence to back up this belief. In **parapsychology** there are documented effects called the experimenter

- What is your name?
- What year it is?
- What is your occupation?
- What is your message?

After the last question leave the recorder running for several minutes. Announce when you are ending the session and turn the recorder off.

You don't need to leave a recorder on for hours to get EVP. In fact two to five minutes of total recording time is enough to get significant results.

Most EVP are short—two to four words in two seconds. EVP often is preceded by a pop or clicking sound. Voices usually sound flat and mechanical. There are computer software programs that can filter background noise to make EVP clearer. Don't over-use computer software, however, because you can distort your results.

You can follow the same procedures in haunted locations.

Don't be discouraged if you get no results, even after trying for a while. EVP is unpredictable, and even the best paranormal investigators don't succeed every time.

effect and the sheep-goat effect. In the experimenter effect the beliefs and expectations of the researcher, even subconscious, will alter results. In the sheep-goat effect believers (sheep) will get more positive results than skeptics (goats). These effects are supported by quantum physics, which supports the interconnectedness of everything. In quantum physics there is no such thing as a separate observer. Even the act of observing influences whatever is being observed.

PHONE CALLS FROM THE DEAD

Phenomena related to EVP include spontaneous phone calls from the dead. In those cases a living person receives a mysterious telephone call from someone who has passed on. The dead person always is the one who makes the call. The line is often full of static and interference, and the voice may be hard to understand or sound odd in some way. However, the voice is recognizable to the receiver. Sometimes the receiver does not know that the caller has died; in other cases, they do know and are shocked to get the call.

Phone calls from the dead are usually short, in which a brief message of farewell or well being is conveyed. The line then goes dead. There are a few cases on record of people carrying on conversations of up to 30 minutes with someone they do not know yet is dead.

WHAT DOES THE FUTURE HOLD?

Researchers envision a time when breakthroughs in technology and consciousness will enable the living to have regular, real-time communication with the dead, extraterrestrials, and ethereals. Imagine a day when you check your phone messages and find several from people who are living and several from people who are dead. In your e-mail box are similar messages from the living and dead, as well as e-mails from beings in other dimensions. And your computer has a new file of helpful information, materialized overnight by spirits who are helping you with your homework or a project. It gives a whole new meaning to the term ghostwriter!

Ghost Hunting with the Pros

Up until the late nineteenth century, ghost hunting was mostly an occasional, amateur pursuit. If unusual activity was reported somewhere, a group of curious persons got together to check it out. Their "investigation" consisted mostly of sitting in the dark waiting for something to happen, or perhaps holding an amateur séance.

Over the last century people and organizations interested in the paranormal have refined ways to investigate ghosts and hauntings. Some ghost organizations offer training programs. Some even have "certification" programs. It is not necessary to be a "certified ghost hunter." Find the ghost groups in your area and attend their meetings. If you like what you see, sign up for their training ghost hunts and workshops. You'll learn the ropes from experienced investigators, and you will get hands-on training.

CAN YOU BE A GOOD GHOST HUNTER?

Ghost hunting can be fun and exciting. Some people think of it as entertainment. However, ghost hunters take their work very seriously. The best of them follow rules and procedures that will help them get useful results.

A real ghost hunt is seldom like the ones portrayed on television and in films. For example, editing eliminates downtime when nothing

Figure 10.1 *The Atlantic Paranormal Society (TAPS) founders Jason Hawes, right, and Grant Wilson set up their digital recording equipment. They host the television show* Ghost Hunters. (Stephen Morton/AP)

happens. In some documentaries, events that have happened over a long period of time are presented together, which can make a haunted place look more active than it is. In truth, ghost hunting is sometimes tedious. You can spend hours and hours hoping something unusual will happen, and nothing does.

So, first and foremost, ghost hunters have to be patient. Sooner or later patience is rewarded. Even a single event, such as mysterious footsteps or an unexplained cold breeze, can make a long evening worthwhile to the ghost hunter.

Besides patience, the other traits of a good ghost hunter include the following:

- *Open-minded but skeptical.* Ghost hunters consider all possible natural causes before they consider the supernatural. Machinery vibrations and lights, road noises, electromagnetic and electrical sources might explain some "ghosts." Eyes can play tricks in the dark. Even people can create mysterious phenomena without real- izing it. For example, someone might cause floorboards to creak. A small number of people deliberately create fraudulent hauntings. They might be looking for publicity, or they might just want to fool with ghost hunters.

- *Good researcher.* Ghost hunters spend a lot of time doing historical research to learn about the background of a haunted place. They read old newspapers, magazines, and public records. They interview eyewitnesses. Ghost hunters also should know as much as possible about ghosts, hauntings, and paranormal phenomena. They study the field. Books, magazines, podcasts, and Web sites offer a wealth of information.

- *Good observer.* If possible, ghost hunters should make more than one visit during both day and night to determine natural lights, shadows, and noises. Maps should be consulted to show fault lines, power lines, and underground streams, mines, and tunnels that might be responsible for a haunting.

- *Good organizer.* Details are important, and can be easy to forget over time. Ghost hunters make careful notes. They organize their reports, photos, recordings, and data so that others can make use of them.

- *Good team player.* Ghost hunts are often organized in groups, under the direction of a leader. Everyone on the team has a job assignment. Ghost hunters must cooperate in order for an investigation to be suc- cessful. Team members work in pairs or small groups, never alone. That way they can double-check each other. It's better to have at least two witnesses.

Borley Rectory: The Most Investigated Haunted Place in History

The gloomy red brick house was built in 1863 to be the home of Reverend Henry Bull, the pastor of Borley Church, located in a lonely country outpost 60 miles northeast of London, England. Borley Rectory should have been a holy place. Instead, it was haunted. Decades later the rectory set off the most celebrated ghost investigation in history.

Legend had it that the rectory was built on the site of an ancient monastery. A nun supposedly was buried there alive as punishment for trying to elope with a monk. While there was no historical record to back up the story, the Bulls did see the ghost of a nun walking about the grounds. A phantom coach driven by headless horsemen also was seen, as were strange lights in the windows of unoccupied rooms.

As hauntings go Borley Rectory was not particularly notable. But when a noted investigator turned his attention to it, the case of the rectory became a sensation. Harry Price almost single-handedly launched the modern era of ghost hunting. Prior to Price most psychical researchers investigated mediums by attending séances. They didn't sit in haunted houses waiting for ghosts to show.

Like many people drawn to the paranormal, Price's interest began when he had an experience in a haunted house at an early age. Later, he joined the Society for Psychical Research in London and made a name for himself investigating fraudulent mediums.

In 1929 Price read about Borley in the newspaper and decided the place should be investigated. The Bulls were no longer there. The new minister was Reverend Lionel Foyster and his wife, Marianne. The Foysters claimed phenomena had gotten much worse. An unknown poltergeist was throwing stones about, ringing bells, and moving objects.

Price was the high-tech man of the times. He had notebooks and pencils for records and sketches; felt shoes for creeping around silently

Figure 10.2 *Borley Rectory in the 1890s.* (Mary Evans Picture Library)

through the house; surgical tape for sealing doors and windows that the ghosts liked to open; a portable telephone for communicating with helpers; a bowl of mercury for detecting tremors in rooms; a remote-controlled cinematograph camera (the forerunner of a video camera); thermometers; graphite for taking fingerprints; cameras with infrared film; chalk for spreading on floors to collect phantom footprints; flashlights; and other items. He even had a flask of brandy on hand in case anyone fainted of fright.

Most ghost hunters today spend a night or two in a haunted place. Price's investigation went on for nine years, from 1929 to 1938. He held séances and communicated with spirits, who made predictions that

(continues)

(continued)

the rectory would burn down. He claimed to document dozens of phenomena, including apparitions, poltergeist effects, spirit writing on walls, and spontaneous combustion.

The haunting drove out the Foysters and their replacements. In 1937 Price rented the rectory for a year to continue his investigation. Strangely—and true to the spirit predictions—a mysterious fire broke out in the rectory in late 1939, and it burned to the ground. The ruins were demolished.

Price and Borley Rectory achieved fame, but critics attacked his work and even accused Price of fabricating some of the things that he claimed to witness. The case remains controversial to this day.

- *Ability to be quiet for long periods of time.* Once equipment is set up and observers are stationed, everyone on a hunt must be quiet—and often very still—for long periods of time. Noise can disrupt hauntings and interfere with the data. If you have a hard time sitting still without fidgeting or talking, practice meditating.

- *Courteous and professional.* Ghost hunters respect the privacy of others. Trespassing can lead to trouble and also harm the reputation of ghost hunting in general. Never vandalize anything or remove "souvenirs" from property. Always dispose of your trash properly or take it home with you. Many private homeowners who ask ghost hunters to visit do not want their homes publicized in the media. Respect their wishes.

HOW A GHOST HUNT IS ORGANIZED

Ghost hunters make arrangements with property owners to have access to a haunted site. Most ghost hunts are done in and around a house or building. Some are outdoors, such as at sacred sites, sites of ruins, and cemeteries. Many cemeteries are privately owned. Responsible ghost hunters do not trespass on private property. Many cemeteries of both private and public ownership are closed at night. Respect the hours posted. Sometimes groups will be given permission to enter after hours.

Once a site has been selected, advance planning is done for how the investigation will be carried out. Groups usually are on site for several hours, sometimes all night. Set-up and breakdown of equipment can take an hour or more at each end. Ideally a team will need at least two hours of quiet time for the actual collection of data.

A lot of advance work can be done during the day. Most ghost-hunting groups like to do their actual investigations at night. Ghostly activity is often higher during nighttime hours, when the waking world is quiet.

A group that ghost hunts on a regular basis develops its own preferred methods of investigation. Most of them fall into three basic types: description, detection, and experimentation.

Description

These activities include careful observations and inspections, note taking, and interviewing eyewitnesses. Some description work should be done prior to the actual investigation.

Some investigators find it helpful to fill out forms. This ensures that investigators will make a note of the same information at all investigations. Always include the following:

- date, time, place
- names of all persons present
- weather conditions (especially important if any work is done outside)
- diagrams of places/rooms investigated
- activities conducted, and by whom

- data collected
- interviews with witnesses
- other notes

Detection

These activities include ways to get measurable data with equipment. (See the section about ghost-hunting tools in this chapter.) Not all work is high-tech, however. Simple detection methods involve spreading of flour, salt, or powder on floors and tables to see if they are disturbed by ghosts. Small objects can be left in certain spots to see if they are moved.

Experimentation

Ghost hunters might have a psychic or medium obtain psychic impressions and perhaps try to communicate with a ghost. Séances are risky unless you know what you're doing. Some investigators try unusual techniques, such as dowsing for ghosts (see description in the next section). Some teams also have on board a demonologist, a person who is experienced in dealing with negative nonhuman presences.

WHAT TOOLS DO YOU NEED?

Ghost-hunting gear ranges from cheap to very expensive. It's nice to have fancy equipment, but you can be a good ghost hunter with simple tools.

Basic tools that all ghost hunters should have are

- notebook and pen for notes and diagrams
- flashlight for seeing in dark places
- camera(s) of preference: 35-mm film, digital, camcorder

- audio recorder for EVP
- tape measure for measuring rooms and sites
- compass for making accurate maps and diagrams
- extra batteries for all equipment
- two-way radios to stay in touch with other team members

Advanced—and more expensive—equipment includes

- **electromagnetic field (EMF) meters,** devices intended to measure geomagnetic storms and measure changes in EMF that might corroborate haunting activity
- tri-field meter, which detects extremely weak static electric and magnetic fields
- field strength meter, which observes radiation patterns of antennae
- night-vision scopes and goggles
- relative humidity gauge, for measuring changes in the air
- negative ion generator, which some investigators believe attracts ghosts
- negative ion detector, for finding areas high in negative, or free, ions, and may reveal explainable sources of such
- Geiger counter, which detects radiation and some anomalous phenomena
- digital thermal scanner, which measures instant changes in temperature
- tremolo meter, a voice-stress analyzer useful for interviewing witnesses, which may reveal possible fraudulent claims
- thermal camera
- motion detector
- oscilloscope for measuring electrical voltage

Seeing Dead People: The Psychic Side of Ghost Hunting

Karl Petry is just like the boy in the film *The Sixth Sense*—he sees dead people, and has since he was a child. When Karl walks into a haunted house, he sees ghosts as though they were living people, only he knows they are dead. He can hear their conversations with each other and know their thoughts and feelings. Sometimes he can even converse with them.

Karl lives in New Jersey, and he is often called to participate in investigations of haunted places. Many ghost hunters know that relying on equipment alone will not give a full picture of a haunting. A good psychic can fill in many details about history, events, and personalities. The information can be researched for accuracy.

When a psychic enters a haunted place, he or she "tunes in" to the surroundings. Impressions flood in. Sometimes psychics even stir up the ghosts, who increase their activity in response to the psychics' presence. The psychic may "see" ghosts and phantom events as mental impressions. Or, as in Petry's case, they may actually see them with their eyes, as though they can peer into another dimension that other people cannot see. The ability to see things that are not part of "normal" reality is called *clairvoyance*, which means "clear seeing."

Psychics also hear sounds that other people cannot hear. For example, they may hear events from the past or hear ghosts talking. This ability is called *clairaudience*, which means "clear hearing."

Psychics sense things with their bodies. They react physically, such as feeling cold or full of electrical energy in certain places. They smell phantom odors. They "know" things about the haunting. This ability is called *clairsentience*, which means "clear sensing."

Kelly Weaver is a medium in Pennsylvania who is highly clairaudient—she hears the voices of spirits and the dead—and she receives mental visual impressions. She also experiences paranormal smells. Spirits and

Figure 10.3 *Psychic Karl Petry can see ghosts as if they were real people.* (Author's collection)

the dead communicate with her through the mental impressions of voices and images.

Everyone has at least some psychic ability. Ghost investigators use their own ability when they get impressions or experience phenomena, such as witnessing an apparition or hearing phantom noises. Psychics have a magnified ability that they have learned to use in a skilled manner.

But no psychic is 100 percent accurate. The impressions they receive are vague or sometimes must be interpreted subjectively. Psychics vary considerably in skill level and in the manner in which they tune in. Nonetheless, they bring a valuable perspective to paranormal investigations.

- laptop computer as a command center
- video monitors for remote viewing

Some investigators develop their own custom setups of equipment, linked to a computer or to cameras or other devices.

WHAT IF YOU DON'T HAVE GEAR?

Although ghost hunters in the media are loaded to the teeth with equipment, it is possible to investigate a haunting with little or no equipment. The earliest ghost hunters had little more than notebooks and film cameras.

The best tool of all is *you*. The human body is an incredible machine for gathering data through the senses: what you see, hear, smell, touch, and even taste. Make lots of notes about everything you observe through all your senses.

Inexpensive models of cameras and audio recorders also can do a good job of getting evidence. You don't necessarily need the top of the line. How you use your equipment will have a great deal to do with your success rate.

DOWSING FOR GHOSTS

If you're adventurous and like to experiment, add a pendulum or dowsing rods to your kit. You will need to learn how to dowse in order to use them. Dowsing is a skill that is part psychic and is used to detect the presence of ghosts.

Dowsing has been used for thousands of years for locating lost and missing persons and animals, and for detecting hidden objects and substances, such as water, oil, coal, minerals, cables, and pipes. Dowsing also is used in the mapping of archaeological sites. No one knows exactly how or why dowsing works. The tool responds to the user. For

Figure 10.4 *This dairy farmer uses dowsing rods to help people find water wells on their property. In paranormal investigations, dowsing rods will move up and down or back and forth when near a particularly haunted area. Rods can also give their holders psychic impressions.* (Bettmann/Corbis)

example, if a dowser is looking for underground water with rods, the rods will signal where the water is by moving up and down or back and forth. A pendulum will begin to whirl. Along with the signals from the tool, the dowser may also get psychic impressions. Some ghost hunters find dowsing helpful for pinpointing the strong areas in a haunted site. Dowsing can also detect unusual fields of geomagnetic energy, which may play a role in hauntings.

Before using dowsing in ghost hunting, first become familiar with your equipment and learn how it responds. Dowsing how-to books explain how to program your rods or pendulum.

Dowsing is fun and unusual. It certainly brings a different angle into a ghost hunt.

KEEP AT IT

Ghost hunting is unpredictable. Sometimes nothing happens. Don't be discouraged if you get no results, even in several ghost hunts. The experience is valuable for training your senses and your ability to collect and analyze data. The more you do it, the more success you will have.

Timeline

Here are some of the notable dates in ghost lore and research referenced in this book:

First century Haunting of Athenodorus, one of the earliest recorded hauntings.

685 Battle of Nechanesmere in Scotland creates ghosts of armies and rescuers.

1642 Battle of Edgehill on October 23, the first intense battle of the English Civil War, leaves ghosts behind.

1642–51 English civil war fought in a series of three conflicts.

1817 Start of the Bell Witch haunting.

1848 Fox sisters hear spirit rappings that fuel the Spiritualism movement.

1856 Manrow House, the "House of Demons" haunting.

1861 Birth of spirit photography by William Mumler.

1862 Battle of Antietam, Maryland on September 17 becomes a ghost battle of the American Civil War.

1861–65 American civil war fought.

1862 Ghost Club founded in London.

1863 Battle of Gettysburg in the American Civil War, fought July 1-3, leaves powerful hauntings behind.

1865 President Abraham Lincoln is assassinated on April 14, and his funeral train from Washington, D.C. to his home in Springfield, Illinois becomes a ghost.

1876 Thomas Marr family banshee appears in West Virginia.

1882 Society for Psychical Research founded in London.

1885 American Society for Psychical Research founded in New York City.

1889 Census of Hallucinations conducted in England and Europe.

1897 Zona Shue is murdered, and her ghosts solves the crime.

1901 Versailles time slip haunting experienced by two Englishwomen.

1905 William Hope becomes a leading photographer of materialized spirits.

1917 Cottingley Fairies fake photographs published in England.

1920 Sir Arthur Conan Doyle says Cottingley Fairies photographs are genuine.

1925 James Chaffin's ghost returns to settle his estate.

1929–38 Harry Price investigates Borley Rectory.

1936 Brown Lady of Raynham Hall, England photographed.

1936 Ghost of Resurrection Mary first seen.

1942 World War II air raid at Dieppe, France becomes a ghost battle.

1959 Friedrich Jurgenson makes breakthroughs in electronic voice phenomena (EVP).

1965–70 Jaboticabal Poltergeist attacks.

1966 Queen's House ghost photographed in Greenwich, England.

1966–67 Mothman hauntings and sightings in West Virginia.

1970s–80s Instrumental transcommunication field of research formed.

1975–76 "Amityville Horror" haunting affects the George Lutz family in Amityville, Long Island, New York.

1980s Cottingley Fairies hoax confessed.

1982 American Association-Electronic Voice Phenomena founded by Sarah Estep.

1991 Ghost girl photographed in Bachelor's Grove Cemetery, Chicago area.

1995 American Ghost Society founded by Troy Taylor.

1999 Ghostvillage.com founded by Jeff Belanger.

2002 *Most Haunted* ghost reality show, produced in England, debuts, featuring medium Derek Acorah and Yvette Fielding.

2004 *Ghost Hunters* reality show, produced in America, debuts, featuring TAPS, The Atlantic Paranormal Research Society.

Glossary

APPARITION   Term usually used by parapsychologists to describe a ghost that is seen. "Apparition" is also applied to visions of the living, such as in cases of apparent bilocation or out-of-body projection, and to visions of religious figures, such as the Virgin Mary.

BANSHEE   A type of death omen ghost found especially in Celtic folklore. Banshees usually are attached to families, have a hideous appearance, and make loud wailing noises when a family member is about to die.

ELECTROMAGNETIC FIELD (EMF) METER   One of the most popular tools of ghost investigators, the EMF meter measures electrical fields in Gauss. If it gives a reading where there are no known EMF sources, it may indicate the presence of ghosts.

ELECTRONIC VOICE PHENOMENA (EVP)   The capturing of spirit voices on audio recorders. The voices usually are not heard until playback.

GHOST   The disembodied form of a dead person or animal; also, the form of an object or structure that no longer exists. Ghosts often are invisible, but when seen can be filmy white and semi-transparent; dark and black; or lifelike. Ghost researchers believe that most ghosts are recordings or imprints, not the actual spirits of the dead.

GHOST RELEASEMENT (ALSO GHOST LAYING)   Various rituals and procedures designed to force a ghost or spirit out of a place are used to release a location from being haunted.

HAUNTING   The presence of a ghost or spirit in a location, such as a house or building, or a place in nature. People who visit a haunted location may become aware of the presence by seeing it, or, more likely, smelling, hearing, or feeling it.

ORBS   Fuzzy balls of light that appear on photographs, especially digital ones. Some people think orbs are ghosts or spirits, but the overwhelming majority of them have natural explanations, such as dust, moisture, or insects that are out of focus.

PARAPSYCHOLOGY   The modern scientific study of paranormal phenomena. Much of the research in parapsychology is done in laboratories, rather than in séance rooms. Some parapsychologists are interested in ghost investigations, but most consider ghost hunting an amateur, nonscientific activity.

POLTERGEIST   A German term that means "noisy spirit." Poltergeists haunt places, and may be human or a spirit or demon. They create disturbances by moving and throwing objects, making foul smells, and causing loud noises. Sometimes they attack the living by biting and scratching.

PSYCHICAL RESEARCH   The scientific study of paranormal phenomena. "Psychical research" is usually applied to activities from the late nineteenth to mid-twentieth centuries. Early psychical researchers focused especially on mediumship and séance-room phenomena.

REVENANT   This old term means ghost or the restless dead.

SÉANCES   A formal attempt by a group of people to communicate with spirits of the dead, séances often involve a medium.

SPECTER   This is an old term for ghost.

SPIRIT PHOTOGRAPHY   The capturing of ghosts and spirits in photographs. The ghosts or spirits usually are not seen when photographs are taken, but show up when the images are developed or viewed.

WHITE NOISE   This background sound is believed to facilitate the manifestation of spirit voices in electronic voice phenomena.

Endnotes

CHAPTER 4

1. Rosemary Ellen Guiley, *The Encyclopedia of Ghosts and Spirits* (New York: Facts On File, 1999), 131.

CHAPTER 5

1. Mark Nesbitt, *The Ghost Hunter's Field Guide: Gettysburg & Beyond* (Gettysburg, Pa.: Second Chance Publications, 2005), 11.

2. Ibid, 12–15.

CHAPTER 6

1. Joshua P. Warren, *Pet Ghosts: Animal Encounters From Beyond the Grave* (Franklin Lakes, N.J.: New Page Books, 2006), 11, 210–211.

CHAPTER 7

1. *Sacramento Union*, October 21, 1856.

CHAPTER 9

1. Rosemary Ellen Guiley, "Death No More A Casket: The EVP Revelations of Sarah Estep," *FATE* 57, no. 12 (December 2004): 21.

Further Research

BOOKS

Belanger, Jeff. *The World's Most Haunted Places*. Franklin Lakes, N.J.: New Page Books, 2004.

An excellent introduction to ghosts. Features an international selection of interesting and noted haunted places.

Guiley, Rosemary Ellen. *The Encyclopedia of Ghosts and Spirits*. New York: Facts On File, 2007.

A comprehensive collection of alphabetical entries on ghost, haunting and poltergeist cases, ghosts in film, Spiritualism and mediumship, psychical research, ghost hunting, afterlife beliefs, and related phenomena. Considered one of the leading books in the field.

Hauck, Dennis William. *The National Directory of Haunted Places*. New York: Penguin, 1996.

More than 2,000 listings of mysterious places in the United States, including hauntings, sacred sites, UFO landing places, sightings of mysterious creatures, and more. Makes an excellent travel companion for taking in the strange on a vacation.

Nesbitt, Mark. *The Ghost Hunter's Field Guide*. Gettysburg, Pa.: Second Chance Publications, 2005.

One of the best ghost-hunting guides available. Nesbitt is an excellent paranormal investigator and the leading expert on ghosts of Gettysburg, Pennsylvania. Especially valuable are the discussions on the why and how of ghosts, plus a great section on ghost-hunting equipment and procedures.

Steiger, Brad. *Real Ghosts, Restless Spirits, and Haunted Places*. Canton, Mich.: Visible Ink Press, 2003.
     A fine compilation of ghost cases, lore, and research by one of the most respected authors of the paranormal. Includes appendices, recommendations on ghost films, and lists of paranormal organizations.

Taylor, Troy. *The Ghost Hunter's Guidebook*. Decatur, Ill.: Whitechapel Productions Press, 2001.
     Taylor, the president and founder of the American Ghost Society, is one of the leading paranormal investigators. This excellent book features the nuts and bolts of everything from ghost tech to using talking boards.

WEB SITES

American Association–Electronic Voice Phenomena
http://www.aaevp.com
Excellent Web site with an international scope on the latest findings in electronic voice phenomena and instrumental transcommunication research and activities. Lots of helpful information on techniques and equipment.

The American Ghost Society
http://www.prairieghosts.com/ags.html
Founder Troy Taylor publishes numerous articles on ghost hauntings and history and offers online courses for all levels of paranormal enthusiasts. His catalog of books and magazines available for sale is one of the best.

Ghostvillage.com

http://www.ghostvillage.com

The largest paranormal Web site on the Internet, founded by Jeff Belanger. Many articles, a free e-newsletter, and lots of networking opportunities are available here.

TAPS (The Atlantic Paranormal Society)

http://www.the-atlantic-paranormal-society.com

TAPS became famous on the reality television show *Ghost Hunters*. The Web site offers a wealth of articles on all aspects of hauntings and other related topics.

Bibliography

Auerbach, Lloyd. *ESP, Hauntings and Poltergeists.* New York: Warner Books, 1986.

Blum, Deborah. *Ghost Hunters: William James and the Search for Scientific Proof of Life After Death.* New York: Penguin, 2006.

Burks, Eddie, and Gillian Cribbs. *Ghosthunter: Investigating the World of Ghosts and Spirits.* London: Headline Book Publishing, 1995.

Butler, Tom F., and Lisa W. *There Is No Death and There Are No Dead: Evidence of Survival and Spirit Communication through Voices and Images from Those on the Other Side.* Reno, Nev.: AAEVP, 2003.

Caidin, Martin. *Ghosts of the Air: True Stories of Aerial Hauntings.* New York: Bantam Books, 1991.

Canning, John, ed. *50 Great Ghost Stories.* New York: Bonanza Books, 1988.

Colombo, John Robert. *Mysterious Canada.* Toronto: Doubleday Canada Ltd., 1988.

Cornell, Tony. *Investigating the Paranormal.* New York: Helix Press, 2002.

Devereux, Paul. *Fairy Paths & Spirit Roads: Exploring Otherworldly Routes in the Old and New Worlds.* London: Vega, 2003.

Doyle, Sir Arthur Conan. *The Coming of the Fairies.* London: Hodder & Stoughton, 1922.

Floyd, E. Randall. *In the Realm of Ghosts and Hauntings: 40 Supernatural Occurrences from around the World.* New York: Barnes and Noble, 2002.

Fodor, Nandor. *On the Trail of the Poltergeist.* New York: The Citadel Press, 1958.

Goss, Michael. *The Evidence for Phantom Hitch-Hikers.* Wellingborough, U.K.: The Aquarian Press, 1984.

Grattan-Guinness, Ivor. *Psychical Research: A Guide to Its History, Principles and Practices.* Wellingborough, U.K.: The Acquarian Press, 1982.

Harper, Charles G. *Haunted Houses: Tales of the Supernatural with Some Accounts of Hereditary Curses and Family Legends.* Rev. and enlarged ed. London: Cecil Palmer, 1924.

Harter, Walter L. *The Phantom Hand and Other American Hauntings.* Englewood Cliffs, N.J.: Prentice-Hall, 1976.

Holzer, Hans. *GHOSTS: True Encounters with the World Beyond.* Chicago: Black Dog and Leventhal Publishers, 1998.

Kaczmarek, Dale. *A Field Guide to Spirit Photography.* Alton, Ill.: Whitechapel Productions Press, 2002.

———. *Illuminating the Darkness: The Mystery of Spook Lights.* Alton, Ill.: Whitechape Productions Press, 2003.

Lysaght, Patricia. *The Banshee: The Irish Supernatural Death Messenger.* Dublin: The Glendale Press, 1986.

Macy, Mark. *Spirit Faces: Truth about the Afterlife.* York Beach, Me.: Red Wheel/ Weiser Books, 2006.

Marsden, Simon. *The Journal of a Ghost Hunter.* London: Little, Brown & Co., 1994.

——— *The Haunted Realm.* Exeter, England: Webb and Bower, 1998.

Nesbitt, Mark. *Ghosts of Gettysburg I-V.* Gettysburg, Pa.: Thomas Publications, 1991–2003.

———. *Ghosts of Gettysburg VI.* Gettysburg, Pa.: Second Chance Publications, 2004.

Owen, A.R.G. *Can We Explain the Poltergeist?* New York: Helix Press / Garrett Publications, 1964.

Price, Harry. *The Most Haunted House in England.* London: Longmans, Green & Co., 1940.

Riccio, Dolores, and Joan Bingham. *Haunted Houses USA.* New York: Pocket Books, 1989

Rogo, D. Scott. *On the Track of the Poltergeist.* Englewood Cliffs, N.J.: Prentice Hall, 1986.

Rogo, D. Scott, and Raymond Bayless. *Phone Calls From the Dead.* Englewood Cliffs, N.J.: Prentice Hall, 1979.

Roll, William G. *The Poltergeist*. Garden City, N.Y.: Doubleday, 1972.

Sheppard, Susan. *Cry of the Banshee: History & Hauntings of West Virginia and the Ohio Valley*. Alton, Ill.: Whitechapel Press, 2004.

Taylor, Troy. *Season of the Witch: The History & Hauntings of the Bell Witch of Tennessee*. Alton, Ill.: Whitechapel Productions Press, 2002.

———. *Ghosts on Film: The History, Mystery & How-To's of Spirit Photography*. Alton, Ill.: Whitechapel Productions Press, 2005.

———. *The Haunted President: The History, Hauntings & Supernatural Life of Abraham Lincoln*. Alton, Ill.: Whitechapel Productions Press, 2005.

Taylor, Troy, and Len Adams. *So, There I Was... More Confessions of Ghost Hunters*. Alton, Ill.: Whitechapel Press, 2006.

Toney, B. Keith. *Battlefield Ghosts*. Berryville, Va.: Rockbridge Publishing Co., 1997.

Underwood, Peter. *Gazetteer of British, Scottish & Irish Ghosts*. New York: Bell Publishing Company, 1985.

Weaver, Kelly with John D. Weaver. *Whispers in the Attic: Living With the Dead*. Camp Hill, Pa.: Spirit House Press, 2004.

Weisberg, Barbara. *Talking to the Dead: Kate and Maggie Fox and the Rise of Spiritualism*. San Francisco: Harper SanFrancisco, 2004.

Wilson, Colin. *Mysteries*. New York: Perigee Books/G.P. Putnam's Sons, 1978.

Index

About the Author and Consulting Editor

ROSEMARY ELLEN GUILEY is one of the foremost authorities on the paranormal. Psychic experiences in childhood led to her lifelong study and research of paranormal mysteries. A journalist by training, she has worked full time in the paranormal since 1983, as an author, presenter, and investigator. She has written 31 nonfiction books on paranormal topics, translated into 13 languages, and hundreds of articles. She has experienced many of the phenomena she has researched. She has appeared on numerous television, documentary, and radio shows. She is also a member of the League of Paranormal Gentlemen for Spooked Productions, a columnist for *TAPS Paramagazine*, a consulting editor for *FATE* magazine, and writer for the "Paranormal Insider" blog. Ms. Guiley's books include *The Encyclopedia of Angels*, *The Encyclopedia of Magic and Alchemy*, *The Encyclopedia of Saints*, *The Encyclopedia of Vampires, Werewolves, and Other Monsters*, and *The Encyclopedia of Witches and Witchcraft*, all from Facts On File. She lives in Maryland and her Web site is http://www.visionaryliving.com.